Practical Pre-School

Role Play

Judith Harries

Contents

Introduction 2
The value of role play 3
Managing role play 5
Links with the Early Learning Goals 9

Role-play scenarios:

The home corner 11

Café/restaurant 14

Health centre 17

Hospital 20

Police station 23

Garage 26

Railway station 29

Supermarket 32

Shoe shop 35

Post office 38

Library 41

Campsite 44

Garden centre 47

Builders' yard 50

Fairy stories 53

Undersea world 56

Bear cave 59

Space rocket 62

Published by Step Forward Publishing Limited St Jude's Church, Dulwich Road, Herne Hill, London, SE24 0PB Tel:020 7738 5454 www.practicalpreschool.com
© Step Forward Publishing Limited 2003   Role Play   ISBN: 1-902438-95-7   ISBN 13: 978 1902 438955
All rights reserved. No part of this publication may be reproduced, stored in a retrieval system, or transmitted by any means, electronic, mechanical, photocopied or otherwise, without the prior permission of the publisher.

Introduction

Role play is a a rich form of play that allows children to explore situations from their own or another person's perspective. It is often an undervalued area of play. This book sets out to explain why it is so important, to offer guidance on managing role play on a daily basis and to give you practical ideas for different scenarios that are both appealing and meaningful for young children.

There are 18 scenarios, many of which can be adapted to create even more. Each one follows a similar format:

What you will need
Each role-play area begins with a comprehensive list of resources. Please don't be daunted by this as lots of areas work with just a few of these ideas. Most children can be relied upon to supply their own imaginative solution when a particular resource is not available. Some basic resources such as screens, drapes and boxes are used in most areas. Others are specific and may be more difficult to come by. Charity shops are a useful source for dressing-up clothes and kitchen items.

Next stop
Many scenarios can be adapted or developed to extend their shelf life by adding new equipment and a different focus, such as opening a pets' corner in the garden centre. Suggestions are included for additions and ideas given for spin-offs that could be set up separately.

Things to make and do
Try to involve the children in preparing a new role-play area whenever possible by making props and resources with you – the more involved they are, the better motivated they will be and the more effective the play. Many of these activities can be done the week before or during the first week as the area develops.

Setting up
Included here are helpful tips on how to build the area. Don't be put off if your setting hasn't got all the equipment mentioned - it's important to be flexible and imaginative. A simple climbing frame can be transformed into a bear cave or a machine with drapes, patience and lots of imagination.

Starting off
This includes suggestions on how to introduce the area to the children along with ideas to stimulate their play activities. Suitable books, fiction and non-fiction, are recommended. It also mentions possible roles children may choose to explore and any safety issues involved in using the area. Where appropriate, ideas are also included for closing or winding down the play area so that the children can be involved from start to finish. It can be disappointing for children to arrive one morning and find the area gone. Make the closure as much a part of the role play as possible – the garage can be demolished to make way for a new supermarket, the library could be closed down and a café built in its place.

Visits and visitors
Most role-play situations benefit from the children's first-hand experience of the real thing through a visit or listening to people who have inside knowledge and experience. This is often an excellent way to introduce a new role-play area.

Outside play
The potential of outside role-play areas is often neglected, possibly because of the unpredictability of our climate, but most areas can include an element of outside play, for instance opening a car wash in the garage.

Home links
The partnership between home and school can be fully exploited through working together on role play. Parents can be involved in collecting resources, sharing expertise and providing opportunities for the children to talk about and continue their play at home. Keep parents informed by sending out a mini-plan every time you change a theme or role-play area. Invite them to give you feedback with observations of what their children have learned.

Early Learning Goals
Each scenario is full of valuable opportunities for children to learn through all six areas of learning and suggestions are given for ideas and activities to develop this. Encourage children to be as independent as possible in their choice of role and use of equipment. Always try to use the children's ideas to spark off conversation and other activities.

The value of role play

Do you make the most of your role-play area? With some thought about the purpose of role play, some careful planning and sensitive intervention, role play can be the most exciting learning experience in your setting.

Every area of the curriculum can be taught through good quality role play. Children can:

- learn to share and take turns;
- use their imaginations;
- explore situations from their own or another person's perspective;
- develop self-confidence and self-esteem;
- express ideas, feelings and anxieties;
- feel valued, listened to and taken seriously;
- learn to collaborate with other children and with adults;
- play a part in observing and assessing both their own and others learning;
- take risks, solve problems and make decisions;
- have the chance to develop their own ideas and explore what they want to know;
- construct and restructure their understanding of the world;
- learn about the culture of others and develop a greater understanding of their own culture;
- learn more about relationships;
- overcome their fears (for example, of the dark or of hospitals or doctors).

The value of play can be seen in children's concentration and the depth of their exploration. Children learn best when they are interested in what they are doing and role play offers that chance for them to become completely absorbed.

Playing is not a break from learning, and there should be rigour in play which demands and challenges children to develop their learning. This means that there needs to be negotiation between adults and children. By working together as partners in planning, proposing and decision-making, you can make both the teaching and learning more productive. Role play provides a link between free and directed play but you need to make sure that positive intervention does not become pointless interfering. Sometimes adults can challenge to invigorate the play and sometimes they can be led by the children and directed by the situation within the play. Role play is the children's domain, and if questions are asked they should be open ended and natural.

There should be intended learning outcomes for role play but be ready to accept that your intentions and the actual learning will not always be the same and to value the learning that does take place.

> The value of role play is nearly always increased if children have had the chance to experience the real situation before the scenario is set up. It may be possible to arrange a visit, for example to your local clinic or shops, and ask permission for the children to talk to some of the staff. Some expert adults are willing to come in and talk to children about their work, demonstrating equipment and techniques.

Role play contributes to the development of learning dispositions and intellectual growth. It promotes a wide

Role Play

range of problem-solving skills. Role-play situations give children the opportunity to develop their understanding of the wider world and of social relationships, so involve them and parents as much as possible in the planning process. Through working together in role play children learn to care for and develop an interest in one another and begin to realise that there are different approaches to learning. They develop a respect for each other, as well as growing in self-confidence and self-awareness.

Role play can take place in many different contexts, with or without props, individually or in a group and may be based on real experiences or fantasy. Different kinds of role play develop different kinds of learning and you need to take advantage of every opportunity for role play, for example using small world equipment such as a dolls' house as well as larger resources.

Children learn different roles in play. They learn to empathise with others by having the opportunity to play at being them, for example, being a dad with two children getting ready to go to the park, someone who people turn to for help, such as a police officer, or someone who needs help, such as a sick child. Some children want to see what it's like to be in charge and become teacher/director, giving you directions or instructions. Some will always want to play a particular role. Through observation you will be able to see whether this is developmental or whether the child needs encouragement and support to move on.

Role play may be continuous and long lasting, for example a child with an imaginary friend. It offers children the time, space and resources to develop ideas which can be ongoing as opposed to tasks which are short and complete. Children need time to 'play themselves out', to return to and refine their play without being told too often that they 'did that yesterday so now do something else today'. Always try to give some indication that it will shortly be time to finish their play and pack up, particularly if they are engrossed in the learning that is taking place.

To make role play valuable you need to show children that you value it. Play is important to children and you need to acknowledge that importance. So make the most of children's wishes to play and follow their lead wherever possible. Plan scenarios together, involve children in discussions about why particular situations may be set up and what to include and, remember, role play can happen anywhere – not just in the role-play area.

Managing role play

Who role plays?

Children may role play on their own, in pairs, in small groups or in large groups. Who is involved in the play changes the dynamics. Role-play situations may allow children to develop relationships with children that they do not usually choose to work with.

Both adults and children need to be involved, but not necessarily in the same ways. Children should sometimes have the opportunity to lead role-play situations without feeling restricted by adults. How children are encouraged to join or persuaded to have a turn can affect the play and their involvement. Some children are not confident about approaching role play and will need encouragement from an adult or their peers. Children instinctively value the importance of play, but some will need more encouragement to be involved than others. Some adults might need help to see that it is not silly and is certainly not a waste of time.

Make sure that all children are able to participate actively within the role-play area. All children should benefit regardless of their gender, ethnicity or ability.

Role play encourages children to develop as individuals and allows both the more and the less able to take part. Differences in children's abilities should not result in a less valuable experience. Role play is ideal for challenging children to develop and enrich their learning because it is dependent upon process rather than a race for a product. Through role play children learn about how to manage differences between people and are able to ask questions and explore this concept.

Bear in mind that the organisation of resources can affect the development of play, particularly for some children, who will not be able to join in if the resources are too cluttered or the furniture is too close together. Other children may feel overwhelmed by the amount of resources or if the resources do not fit in with their particular way of learning. Talk with the children about the resources they want to use and about why they are necessary. Children will come up with their own ideas for resources and both you and the children need to feel comfortable with them in order to develop learning.

You may want to restrict numbers of children in the role-play area because of safety considerations or to give more opportunity to those children who would otherwise not choose that situation. You may, occasionally, choose who can use the role-play area. This may be to redress a gender imbalance or to give more opportunity to less confident children. You need to decide whether children always choose the grouping or to what extent you intervene.

Think about your own involvement. Practitioners are often concerned about the extent to which role play is engineered or orchestrated. Adults have a role in stimulating play ideas and developing understanding and possibilities. They may be involved in a number of ways, for example:

- as fellow role players, sometimes leading and sometimes being directed by the children;
- as observers;
- providing a new perspective.

Children may need to be challenged in order to move on and develop the play. At times they will repeat play activities and by doing so may consolidate their learning. However, repetitive play without development can hinder learning. Sensitive adult intervention is really important at this stage.

Think about

- How children get involved in planning a situation and, if they have, are they then more interested in being the ones who use it?
- When role play takes place outside any defined area or situation. Is it part of a story, daily contact, in conversation or incidental?
- Do children play more when they can choose the context, time and the grouping?
- Are they more interested, and is play developed differently, if the children choose the activity rather than you?
- Do children return - or are they encouraged to return - to refine, conclude, or develop play situations?

Role Play

Where and when to role play

Role play doesn't have to take place in a role-play area - you don't want to dictate that 'We read here' and 'We role play there'. It can happen spontaneously anywhere and you need to be aware of that and be ready to respond. It can happen as a result of a story or poem or because of something that a child has said or brought in. However, contructing role-play situations is important in giving children the opportunity to develop understanding of the wider world and of social relationships, and often children feel more secure if the area is clearly defined.

Role play doesn't have to be sophisticated and realistic, it may just need an object to hand and a good idea. Children may use real objects to represent another object - a washing basket can become a dog's kennel, a boat or a bird's nest. It is the process of learning and exploration that is important rather than having exactly the right equipment.

Some practitioners are concerned about the facilities and space they have for role play, especially if the premises are shared with other users. What about working with children to create an area as part of the play? You could use wooden cubes or big building blocks as a space divider.

Create role-play situations indoors and outdoors. Different sorts of role play are possible outside, for example, making mud pies to decorate and sell or using wheeled vehicles when setting up a garage. Large tabards can be made to go over outdoor coats for dressing up. Have ready-made signs and posters and portable sacks, screens and cases full of props to create a role-play area instantly.

Try to encourage role play alongside adult areas - an adult meeting area, a secretary's area, a safe food and drink area - so that adults and children are working alongside one another at the same time. You'll find that the modelling and conversations are different.

Think about whether children can have free access to the role-play situation or whether there are only certain times within the day that it will be available to them. You should also be sensitive to children's individual needs – sometimes children will need their own space, sometimes they will want to work alongside a friend and sometimes they are happy to be part of a group. In the role-play situation, where there tend to be fewer rules, it is important to observe children closely so that you can see when children are struggling and how best to intervene.

How to role play

Role play can be an extremely exciting way for children to learn, but to be most beneficial it needs to be well managed and organised. Resources must be appropriate and valued by both adults and children. You must also think about how you will give children access to resources - whether or not all of the resources will be available all of the time and where they will be kept.

Adults and children should discuss the physical limitations of the space available and how this can best be used, particularly at the start of the project when there will be a great deal of excitement and interest by large numbers of children. This enthusiasm needs to be managed so that it is not diminished but makes a positive contribution to the development of the role-play situation. A well-developed role-play situation is likely to influence work going on throughout the setting and you will need to plan for this.

Whether children or adults initiate role play there is always a framework to it and usually rules that provide a structure. Children can be involved in the planning stage of developing the framework, for example, agreeing whether there should be a limit on the number of children involved at any one time. Should there be any rules regarding care of the role-play environment? How long should the situation last? It is useful for children to know this at the start. You could explain, for example, that you plan to set it up for two weeks at first and then you'll talk about whether they want to change anything, add more equipment or whether they have learned what they hoped to learn and want to change it completely.

Role play is attractive to children because there are no right or wrong answers. It allows for exploration, giving breadth and depth to learning.

Children may role play for all kinds of reasons: to play in parallel or with others; to make sense of a situation; to forget a worry; to practise negotiation; to dominate or be told what to do; to tell a story; to imitate the adults' world; to rationalise emotions; or just for their enjoyment. But how do they get involved? Is it because they are asked by an adult or another child; by being given a turn; by being told they can play there after they've done something more important; by seeing that it is an exciting and attractive place to be?

Think about

- Whether role play is something which happens just in the role-play area (however many times it changes from a hairdresser's to a vet's)?

- Do you encourage and give children time to set up their own fantasy play around their other play? Can children return to their play? Time is a factor because children's play often remains at the organisational stage and the opportunity to genuinely develop the fantasy is cut short.

- How much modelling and role play do adults do? Do children see you playing in role with other adults? For example, sometimes as teacher, as colleague, friend or even parent?
- How do children play with others and how do adults develop, modify or enrich the play? When adults are used to joining in with the play they are often included by the children. In settings where adults never role play the children's play doesn't naturally involve an adult because they know the play is restricted to something only children do.
- How are children involved in setting up or developing their role-play environments? What help, support and resources are available for them?

Your role
- Discriminatory behaviour and attitudes must be challenged.
- Play allows for discussion and explanation. Adults need to listen to children's points of view as well as giving their own.
- Violence against self, others or the environment is not appropriate but children need to learn to express anger and a variety of emotions in appropriate ways. You should enable children to experience and give a name to a whole range of emotional responses in role play by developing situations which encourage children to say how they feel within a 'safe' environment.
- Children may wish to bring their own toys into the role-play situation, for example, toy guns. You and your colleagues need to have a common response to this so that children are not confused and adults can explain their response.

Role play needs to be a planned experience. However, it is not a race through curriculum content. Allow time for investigation and thinking. The process of play is learner-orientated and children often surprise us with their connections and developments.

It is important to have expectations of the learning outcome from role play and to share these with the children. The children may have their own expectations and be able, through practice, to pinpoint their learning or the learning of others. This development comes through talking with the children about learning on a regular basis.

Role play gives children freedom to express their own understanding and their attitudes. You need to be aware of the possible need to respond to inappropriate social behaviour. Discrimination and stereotyping will need to be challenged and explored with children.

Some adults may choose to positively discriminate for boys and for girls. For example, having a boys only time in the home corner or having a girls only time with the wheeled toys outside. In this way you may help to redress the balance of learning. However, this will need discussion with both children and families in order to gain understanding about the reasons behind this, and will need to be carefully observed by adults to monitor the consequences.

Adults need to encourage children to challenge gender stereotypes in role play so that children can then transfer this understanding to other areas of learning.

Cultural diversity
It is not only tangible resources that affect children's learning but also the attitudes and beliefs of those with whom the children are working. Role-play situations are often a good setting in which to explore this hidden curriculum and to make it explicit rather than implicit.

Be aware that your assessment and role play may be biased towards one particular culture. Ask yourself how this can be redressed and how the learning of all children may be valued.

You may use role play to introduce children to the rich diversity of cultures. Children will need time to explore and to talk about differences and similarities between their own culture and those of others.

Be aware of the danger of stereotyping. For example Chinese utensils and costumes should not only be available at the time of Chinese New Year. There should be references to a wide variety of cultures as part of all role-play situations.

It is vital that adults promote questioning and stimulate debate about cultural diversity through the role-play situation.

There are many differences between children of the same ethnic background. They will have different interests, different approaches to learning and bring with them different experiences. Children need to be valued as individuals.

Home links
Good communication with parents and carers is important if children are to benefit from their understanding and participation. Children and their families should be involved in planning the role-play situation and encouraged to contribute to ideas. In this way, you can make sure that it is culturally sensitive and not likely to cause offence.

Welcome the objects that children bring from home and make sure that they are treated with respect by others.

Inform families and talk to children about the learning intentions of the role-play situation and the benefits to the children.

Families may need encouragement to take an active part in the role play alongside their child or as an observer.

Equipment and materials
Some of the best role play can take place with a box, a blanket and a torch. Occasionally, no equipment at all is

Role Play

needed; the resource is the children's minds. Children use resources in an imaginative way, for example, a hairbrush can become a microphone. When resources are used they should be appropriate and valued by both the adult and the child.

Make sure that the emphasis is on creating environments to promote high quality learning rather than creating environments of high quality resources. Quality can be destroyed by the reactions of other people and this can even make play a painful experience.

Think about how children will access the resources they need. Children and adults working together may need to decide what resources will be available and where they will be kept. There needs to be some discussion about the care of resources, leading to an understanding of social responsibility. Through role play children learn to share their resources with other people.

Through observation of children's learning adults may wish to add resources or to take away resources in order to develop that learning further. Some of the resources in the role-play situation may be unfamiliar and should promote questions and a sense of wonder.

Children may wish to bring some additional resources from home that may be appropriate in the role-play situation. These need to be carefully introduced to all the children working in that area and need to be shown value by both adults and children.

Children will have their own ideas as to which resources would be appropriate. When a role-play situation is decided upon, children can use reference books to plan the resources they think they need. Some of these children will then become experts on particular items and a resource for other children.

You need to provide appropriate resources that are culturally sensitive to the situation and to the children and families within the setting. Use appropriate language to describe the resources and be aware of their use within the context.

Observing role play

Children have an enormous capacity for learning. Observation can reveal children's learning potential as well as what they have already learned. What children can already do should be the starting point for planning the next step. Practitioners can only know what children can already do by careful observation. Observation must be planned and carried out with sensitivity and respect.

It may be useful to observe children with specific questions in mind. For example, you may be interested in observing their social skills or their literacy skills. You may want to compare this observation with those done in other areas of the setting. Do children display more knowledge and understanding in role play than in the maths corner?

Observation needs organisation. It should be part of everyday work and then time set aside for reflection. It is useful to have a number of different people observing during the course of a day or a week so that these can be compared and contrasted.

Children are also able to observe and have quite definite ideas about how they and their peers are learning. This can be a useful contribution to add to the observations made by the adult.

Children bring their own agendas to role play. For example, playing out the feelings of being rejected when a new baby is born. You can discover much about children's thoughts and therefore plan to support them.

The things that children reveal in their play are often far more sophisticated than the answer they will give to a question that is posed by an adult. They perform better when the pressure of getting something right or wrong or the desire to please is removed.

Recording provides the evidence of what children are learning and allows us to analyse this learning and to feed it into planning. Recording should be about dispositions of learning as well as skills, knowledge and concepts.

Collecting evidence of children's learning

Play gives children confidence. It allows children to remain in control of their own learning. As a result, children are able to demonstrate their breadth and depth of learning through role play.

Play is not easily measured. However, assessing and evaluating children's learning through role play is essential in understanding what children have already learned and in planning the next steps for their learning.

You need to collect evidence of learning in children's play without controlling the play situation. Bear in mind the possible learning outcomes, but be prepared for children to develop their learning in unexpected ways.

Often children develop skills, knowledge and understanding through the play situation that they then transfer to other areas of the curriculum. Be aware of this and look at the transferability of skills.

You will need time to observe children at play. This time needs to be valued by all members of the team and planned into the everyday working.

Intervention in role play needs to be sensitive and the assessment needs to evaluate the effectiveness of the role of the adult, as well as the match between the curriculum and the child.

Naomi Compton, head of early years and childcare, Derbyshire and Sheila Sage, early years inspector, Worcestershire.

Links with the Early Learning Goals

To help you with your planning, all of the activities suggested for each role-play area are listed under the six areas of learning. The codes in brackets show which Early Learning Goals the activities promote.

These pages highlight parts of the *Curriculum Guidance for the Foundation Stage* in point form to show what children are expected to be able to do in each area of learning by the time they enter Year 1. These points are used throughout this book to show how activities link to these expectations. For example, Personal, Social and Emotional Development point 7 is 'form good relationships with adults and peers'. Activities suggested which provide the opportunity for children to do this will have the reference PS7.

Personal, Social and Emotional Development (PS)

This area of learning covers important aspects of development that affect the way children learn, behave and relate to others. By the end of the Foundation Stage, most children will:

PS1 continue to be interested, excited and motivated to learn

PS2 be confident to try activities, initiate ideas and speak in a familiar group

PS3 maintain attention, concentrate and sit quietly when appropriate

PS4 have a developing awareness of their own needs, views and feelings and be sensitive to the needs, views and feelings of others

PS5 have a developing respect for their own cultures and beliefs and those of other people

PS6 respond to significant experiences, showing a range of feelings when appropriate

PS7 form good relationships with adults and peers

PS8 work as part of a group or class, taking turns and sharing fairly, understanding that there needs to be agreed values and codes of behaviour for groups of people, including adults and children, to work together harmoniously

PS9 understand what is right, what is wrong, and why

PS10 dress and undress independently and manage their own personal hygiene

PS11 select and use activities and resources independently

PS12 consider the consequences of their words and actions for themselves and others

PS13 understand that people have different needs, views, cultures and beliefs, that need to be treated with respect

PS14 understand that they can expect others to treat their needs, views, cultures and beliefs with respect

Communication, Language and Literacy (L)

The objectives set out in the National Literacy Strategy: Framework for Teaching for the Reception year are in line with these goals. By the end of the Foundation Stage, most children will be able to:

L1 enjoy listening to and using spoken and written language, and readily turn to it in their play and learning

L2 explore and experiment with sounds, words and texts

L3 listen with enjoyment and respond to stories, songs and other music, rhymes and poems and make up their own stories, songs, rhymes and poems

L4 use language to imagine and recreate roles and experiences

L5 use talk to organise, sequence and clarify thinking, ideas, feelings and events

L6 sustain attentive listening, responding to what they have heard by relevant comments, questions or actions

L7 interact with others, negotiating plans and activities and taking turns in conversation

L8 extend their vocabulary, exploring the meaning and sounds of new words

L9 retell narratives in the correct sequence, drawing on language patterns of stories

L10 speak clearly and audibly with confidence and control and show awareness of the listener, for example by their use of conventions such as greetings, 'please' and 'thank-you'

L11 hear and say initial and final sounds in words and short vowel sounds within words

L12 link sounds to letters, naming and sounding letters of the alphabet

L13 read a range of familiar and common words and simple sentences independently

L14 show an understanding of the elements of stories such as main character, sequence of events, and openings, and how information can be found in non-fiction texts to answer questions about where, who, why and how

L15 know that print carries meaning, and in English, is read from left to right and top to bottom

L16 attempt writing for different purposes, using features of different forms such as lists, stories and instructions

L17 write their own names and other things such as labels and captions and begin to form sentences, sometimes using punctuation

L18 use their phonic knowledge to write simple regular words and make phonetically plausible attempts at more complex words

L19 use a pencil and hold it effectively to form recognisable letters, most of which are correctly formed

Mathematical Development (M)

The key objectives in the National Numeracy Strategy: Framework for Teaching for the Reception year are in line with these goals. By the end of the Foundation Stage, most children should be able to:

M1 say and use number names in order in familiar contexts

M2 count reliably up to ten everyday objects

M3 recognise numerals one to nine

M4 use language such as 'more' or 'less' to compare two numbers

M5 in practical activities and discussion begin to use the vocabulary involved in adding and subtracting

M6 find one more or one less than a number from one to ten

M7 begin to relate addition to combining two groups of objects and subtraction to 'taking away'

M8 talk about, recognise and recreate simple patterns

M9 use language such as 'circle' or 'bigger' to describe the shape and size of solids and flat shapes

M10 use everyday words to describe position

M11 use developing mathematical ideas and methods to solve practical problems

M12 use language such as 'greater', 'smaller', 'heavier' or 'lighter' to compare quantities

Knowledge and Understanding of the World (K)

By the end of the Foundation Stage, most children will be able to:

K1 investigate objects and materials by using all of their senses as appropriate

K2 find out about, and identify, some features of living things, objects and events they observe

K3 look closely at similarities, differences, patterns and change

K4 ask questions about why things happen and how things work

K5 build and construct with a wide range of objects, selecting appropriate resources and adapting their work where necessary

K6 select the tools and techniques they need to shape, assemble and join materials they are using

K7 find out about and identify the uses of everyday technology and use information and communication technology and programmable toys to support their learning

K8 find out about past and present events in their own lives, and those of their families and other people they know

K9 observe, find out about and identify features in the place they live and the natural world

K10 begin to know about their own cultures and beliefs and those of other people

K11 find out about their environment, and talk about those features they like and dislike

Physical Development (PD)

By the end of the Foundation Stage, most children will be able to:

PD1 move with confidence, imagination and in safety

PD2 move with control and coordination

PD3 show awareness of space, of themselves and of others

PD4 recognise the importance of keeping healthy and those things which contribute to this

PD5 recognise the changes that happen to their bodies when they are active

PD6 use a range of small and large equipment

PD7 travel around, under, over and through balancing and climbing equipment

PD8 handle tools, objects, construction and malleable materials safely and with increasing control

Creative Development (C)

By the end of the Foundation Stage, most children will be able to:

C1 explore colour, texture, shape, form and space in two or three dimensions

C2 recognise and explore how sounds can be changed, sing simple songs from memory, recognise repeated sounds and sound patterns and match movements to music

C3 respond in a variety of ways to what they see, hear, smell, touch and feel

C4 use their imagination in art and design, music, dance, imaginative and role play and stories

C5 express and communicate their ideas, thoughts and feelings by using a widening range of materials, suitable tools, imaginative and role play, movement, designing and making, and a variety of songs and musical instruments

The home corner

Everybody knows what to expect in the home corner. Here are some simple ways to develop play by ringing the changes and celebrating special events and occasions with the children.

What you will need

For dressing up – boys' and girls' clothes, including multicultural outfits

Cooking and eating utensils

Food – plastic, salt dough, real

Ornaments

Mirror

Potted plant

Books, magazines

Telephone, directories

Dolls, cot, bedding

Money, bags, umbrella

Furniture – bed, bedding, pillow, cushions, Hoover, television, comfy chairs, washing machine, iron and ironing board, table and chairs, cooker, microwave, fridge, sink, toaster

Tape recorder

Special events

New baby – extra dolls, new baby dolls, baby clothes, nappies, baby wipes, toys, bottles, food, high chair, pushchair, Moses basket, baby bath, towel, changing mat, camera, new baby wrapping paper, nursery wallpaper.

Birthday party – party clothes, dressing-up clothes for entertainer (clown suit, magician's cape and hat), paper cups, plates, serviettes, straws, tablecloth, presents (see 'Things to make and do'), cards, wrapping paper, sticky tape, scissors, empty boxes, birthday cake, party food, candles, balloons, streamers, party poppers, party music, invitations, camera.

Wedding reception – bridal clothes, bouquets, fancy clothes, hats, gloves, shoes, jewellery, rings, tablecloths, flower arrangements for table, fancy food, presents, camera, tripod, photo albums, wedding magazines.

House at night – pyjamas, dressing gowns, slippers, toothbrushes, storybooks, duvets, blankets, clock, black-out curtains for windows, silver stars, curtains, working lamps, torches, television, TV magazines, newspapers.

Terrace/row of houses – share furniture between houses, set of cooking and eating utensils for each house with matching colour or pattern, different coloured front doors and house numbers, different occupations for each family, paper, envelopes.

Festival boxes - a box of extra resources to transform the home corner.

Christmas – party clothes, tree, decorations, advent calendar, special food, stockings, fireplace, presents, cards, fairy lights, Christmas music.

Diwali – Indian dressing-up clothes, pictures of Diwali celebrations, clay divas, candles, tea lights, fairy lights, chalk for rangoli patterns, mendhi and pattern book, Diwali cards, Indian cooking utensils and recipes, Indian music.

Chinese New Year – Chinese dressing-up clothes, pictures of New Year celebrations, Chinese cooking utensils and recipes, red envelopes, red cushions, serviettes, and curtains, Chinese music and dragon.

Things to make and do

Make pretend presents. Wrap different-sized boxes in suitable wrapping paper for the special event. Remind children not to unwrap them!

Make special cakes for special occasions from an empty cake tin, covered in papier mache or Modroc and painted. Attach a cake frill made from crepe paper. Add real candles.

Role Play

Stick new baby, birthday, wedding or Christmas wrapping paper on a screen as a backdrop.

Setting up
The home corner will take on the character and atmosphere of each special event if you can supply some of these resources. Try keeping the resources for different special events in a separate box so the children can unpack them and be involved in setting up, or putting away, the home corner.

Starting off
Explain to the children that the home corner is to have a new special emphasis.

Read an appropriate storybook such as *This is Jane, Jim* by Kaye Umansky (Red Fox) or *Kipper's Birthday Party* by Mick Inkpen (Hodder). Use the children's own experiences and memories to introduce the different scenarios.

Safety Take care when using real candles. Help children to be aware of leads and wires attached to any electrical equipment used in the house such as tape recorders, fairy lights, and lamps. Warn them not to touch plugs or lights.

Roles Family member, adult, child, friend, visitor, neighbour, childminder, postman, milkman, refuse collector, window cleaner, mobile hairdresser, pizza delivery person, meter reader, painter and decorator.

Visits and visitors
Invite a parent with a new baby to come and talk to the children about all the things you need to look after a new baby.

Invite people from a variety of cultures to come and share with the children how they celebrate different festivals.

Outside play
Don't forget the garden! Try to provide the children with an area outside that they can use as a garden attached to the home corner. Plant out new plants and vegetables in the spring. Weed and water the garden regularly. Take photos of guests at parties in the garden. Hang up washing on the line. Provide play equipment, balls, hoops and a sandpit.

Home links
Keep parents informed of changes to the home corner so that they can support you with resources and talk to their children at home about their play.

Hold a real party in the nursery to celebrate a special event, anniversary or festival. The children can use skills they have practised in role play to help plan and organise the party.

Personal, Social and Emotional Development
Talk about baby brothers and sisters. How does it feel to have a new baby in the house? What could the children do to help? (PS1, 2, 4, 6)

Ask children to think about parties they have been to. Work as a group to plan a party for the home corner, making lists of guests, food, and games. (PS2, 6, 8)

What could go wrong at a party? Act out some of the children's ideas - nobody turns up, there's a power cut, mum drops the cake, a favourite present gets broken, and so on. (PS4, 6)

Children can work together to tidy up after a celebration. Who will wash the dishes and Hoover the carpet? (PS8)

Share a cosy snack time in the night house. Cuddle up in pyjamas with hot chocolate to drink and cookies to eat, and listen to a bedtime story. (PS7, 8)

Communication, Language and Literacy

Phone friends and neighbours to come to a party and celebrate. 'Please come to my birthday party tomorrow.' (L1, 4, 5, 10)

Phone the florist or caterer to order things for the party. (L1, 4, 5, 7)

Make a book of favourite party games or special recipes. (L5, 7, 14, 16)

Write invitations to guests, and thank-you letters for birthday or wedding presents. (L16, 17)

Make name cards for the party table. (L17)

Mathematical Development

Set the table for a party of eight. 'I have seven plates. I need one more.' 'Can you put a straw in each cup?' (M1, 2, 6)

Say the rhyme 'Five little candles' (*This Little Puffin*) at the birthday party. (M1, 2, 4)

The postman has cards to deliver to house numbers 2 and 3. Can he find the right house? (M3)

'I have a new baby sister. There are five people in my family now.' (M5, 6)

Phone up for a take-away. 'Please can we have three pizzas at number 30. It's next to the garage.' (M1, 2, 10, 11)

Knowledge and Understanding of the World

Bake a birthday cake or decorate little cakes with coloured icing. (K3, 4)

Take photos of a party or wedding reception and display them on the wall or in an album. (K7)

Invite children to talk about special events or parties they have enjoyed with their families. Bring in photos and artefacts to share. (K8, 10)

Look at technology used in the kitchen and home corner. How do the different appliances work? (K4, 7)

What do the children like and dislike about the home corner? How could it be improved? (K9, 11)

Physical Development

Play party games such as musical bumps and statues. (PD1, 2, 3)

Use 'sit and ride' toys to deliver goods to the home corner such as milk, pizzas and parcels, and take rubbish away. (PD2, 6)

Pretend to be a window cleaner or painter and climb ladders and stretch up high to make the house ready for a party. (PD1, 2, 8)

Move carefully around the house with the lights on. Try again in the house in the dark. (PD1, 3)

Creative Development

Print wrapping paper using potato or vegetable prints on sugar paper. Make repeating patterns using hearts and horseshoes (wedding), trees and bells (Christmas), baby rattles (new baby). (C1)

Sing songs in the house: 'Rock a bye baby', 'Happy birthday', and Christmas carols. (C2)

Sing 'Do you know the muffin man?' and change it to other visitors, for example milkman, postman, dustman. (C2)

Listen to music from around the world in the home corner. How does it make you feel? Can you dance to it? (C2, 3)

Make salt dough food for the party – fancy cakes and biscuits, sausage rolls and jam tarts, samosas and pancake rolls. (C5)

Design and make cards for a new baby, birthday, wedding, Christmas and other festivals. (C5)

Café or restaurant

Working and eating out in the role-play café or restaurant appeals to most children, especially if you can combine it with cooking and eating real food! Suitable themes include 'Food', 'Seasons' and 'Materials'.

> Adapt to be a hotel or pizza delivery service

What you will need

For dressing up – uniforms, aprons, chef's hat

Several small tables and chairs

Tablecloths, napkins, vases and flowers

Plates, bowls, cups and saucers, glasses

Knives, forks and spoons

Notepad and pencil

Printed menus

Cooking utensils, pots and pans

Cooker, sink, fridge, play kitchen furniture

Telephone

Cash till, money

Leaflets advertising cafés

Food – plastic, salt dough (see below) and real!

Fast food option – take-away boxes and cups. Most fast food outlets will supply you with a selection of these on request.

Ingredients for cooking

Next stop

Add on a bedroom, provide luggage and open a hotel.

Add a pizza delivery service with bicycle or scooter, helmet, boxes, menu and street map.

Close down the restaurant due to staff holidays, for redecoration or too many complaints and disastrous environmental health inspections!

Things to make and do

Make pretend food using a variety of materials – salt dough biscuits, cakes, sausages and chicken legs.

Cut cakes and chips out of yellow sponge foam.

Make pizzas from cardboard circles and collage materials.

Make favourite meals using paper plates, photos of food from magazines, or collage materials.

Setting up

Decide with children what sort of café they want to set up – fast food take-away or sit down at tables. Do they want fish and chips, Chinese or Indian food, pizzas, a tea shop or a posh restaurant? There are lots of options!

Use two or three small tables, laid out with tablecloths and place settings.

Use a portable screen to separate off a kitchen area and arrange kitchen furniture.

Starting off

Talk to children about their experiences of eating out. These will vary enormously. Read *The Tiger who Came to Tea* by Judith Kerr (Collins). What do they like/not like about eating in a café?

Explain that you are opening the café on a certain day. Ask children to come dressed up, if appropriate. Provide some real food to share in the café.

Safety Take care not to rush around when people are carrying trays/drinks.

Roles Manager, waiter/waitress, head chef, sous chef, dishwasher, customer.

Visits and visitors

Many cafés are happy to show children around and talk about the work they do, so arrange a visit before setting up the role-play area. Often supermarkets will let you visit their café area.

Invite parents/carers who work in catering to talk to the children about their work. Alternatively, you could invite a vegetarian or farmer to talk about their views on food.

Outside play

Set up the café outside on a sunny day and use tables with umbrellas, or an awning. How could the children change the menu to suit the hot weather?

Find a suitable place nearby for a picnic and invite children and their families to enjoy a picnic lunch together.

Home links

Organise a fundraising event. Open a tea shop after school one day and invite families to buy biscuits and cakes made by the children. With parents' help children can also be involved in serving drinks.

Ask parents to talk to children about eating out and visit a café together if possible. Be sensitive about how much families can afford.

Invite children and parents to write or record reviews of where they have eaten out. Issue star ratings for local cafés based on child-friendly considerations.

Personal, Social and Emotional Development

If everyone wants to be the chef, or the waitress, you may need to discuss the need for different roles. The café won't be as much fun without customers! (PS1, 8)

How will the children make customers feel welcome? How do they like to be treated? (PS4, 6)

Talk about food from a variety of cultures. Organise a special French, Italian or Spanish day. Change the café into an Indian or Chinese restaurant. (PS5)

How should you behave when eating out? How will the café cope with a badly behaved child who is rude to the waiter and spills her food on purpose? (PS9, 12)

Talk about personal hygiene in the café and when cooking at nursery. Why is it important to wash your hands before handling food? (PS10)

Find out about traditions associated with food and eating in different cultures, festivals and seasons. Hold a special celebration in the café for a birthday or festival. (PS13, 14)

Communication, Language and Literacy

Encourage lots of conversation and use of appropriate language. 'Why don't you try the chicken? Then we could share a piece of chocolate fudge cake.' 'What would you like to drink?' 'Please can I have a chocolate milkshake?' 'Certainly, sir.' (L1, 4, 10)

Does the waiter listen carefully and get the order right, or not? (L4, 5, 6)

Extend vocabulary by learning new words for food and utensils. (L8)

Follow recipes and retell to each other in the kitchen. 'Let's make pasta. You need onions, tomatoes and then cheese.' (L9)

Write notices and signs – 'Welcome', 'Toilet', 'Exit', and 'Kitchen'. Plan, type and print out menus for café tables. Use words and diagrams. Write out 'Specials' on a chalkboard. (L11, 12, 13, 16)

Look at cookery books to introduce children to following instructions. (L14)

Let the waiter use a notepad and pencil to take down orders and write out bills and receipts. (L16, 19)

Write comments for a suggestion box, complimenting or complaining about food, service, and so on.

Mathematical Development

Invent a phone number for the café. Write it out and stick it on the phone. Children can answer the phone and take bookings. '875226. A table for four at 7.30? What's your name madam?' Use *Yellow Pages* to find other numbers for cafés. (M1, 3)

Encourage children to count. 'How many people want soup?' 'Are there enough wine glasses at this table?' (M2)

Do some cooking for the café and give children practical experience, measuring and weighing ingredients. (M4, 12)

'There are five people at the table. Here are four cakes. You need one more.' (M4, 5, 6)

Decorate cakes and pizzas with patterns and sell them in the café. (M8)

'We need a bigger table. Have you got a round table?' 'Can I have a smaller helping of ice cream, please?' (M9, 12)

The waiters got tips of £2.00. Can they share it out? (M11)

Knowledge and Understanding of the World

In practical cookery sessions, enjoy the smell of the food, the feel of different ingredients, the sounds of spoons stirring and electric mixers whizzing and the sight and taste of the finished recipe. (K1, 3)

Make real cakes, jam tarts, scones and biscuits to sell in the tea shop (see 'Home links'). (K1, 2, 3, 4)

Look at the different utensils we use when cooking – glass bottles, metal spoons, plastic bowls, wooden chopping boards. (K2, 3, 4)

Use an electric mixer and a fork or hand whisk to mix eggs. Which is the most efficient? Make meringues to sell in the café. (K2, 3)

Plan menus for different seasons. What will people want to eat in the café in winter? (K4)

Cooking uses lots of different technology. Talk about microwaves, fridges, timers, mixers and blenders. (K6, 7)

What do you like or dislike about the café? How could the atmosphere be improved? 'We need some music to listen to.' (K11)

Physical Development

Children will need to take care when carrying trays of food and crockery. Have fun carrying a full tray around the balancing equipment. (PD1, 6, 7)

Is there room in the café to move around without knocking over people or tables? Could a wheelchair get about the café? (PD2, 3)

Some activities require a fine degree of control – cracking an egg, mixing a cake, stacking a tray and carrying a full glass. (PD2)

Is the food in the café healthy or not? What is wrong with too much fast food? (PD4)

How does it feel when you are hungry, or full up after a big meal? Why do you need a drink when you've been exercising? (PD5)

Handle kitchen utensils carefully, especially knives for chopping ingredients and electric mixers. (PD8)

Creative Development

Look at paintings of café scenes by Renoir and Degas. Ask children to paint pictures of people eating lots of different sorts of food to hang on the walls of the café. (C1)

Sing 'Pizza hut' from *Popocatepetl* (Sing for Pleasure). (C2)

Make kitchen music using utensils from the café. (C2)

Encourage children to talk about what they see, hear, smell, touch and taste in the café. (C3)

Experiment with playdough. Add seeds, beads, sequins and pasta to make different textures. Make strange biscuits to sell at the café. What will they be called? Do they have magical qualities? (C4, 5)

Be dramatic. Complain about your meal. 'This food is revolting. I want my money back!' How do the waiter, chef and manager respond? (C5)

Work in pairs and role play different characters. Choose two roles out of the hat such as slow waiter and impatient customer, or angry manager and late waitress. (C5)

Use a camcorder to film customers leaving the café. Interview them for the local news. Did they enjoy their meal? (C5)

Health centre

> Adapt to be a doctor's, dentist, optician's or a baby clinic

This is a useful way of combining several familiar role-play situations under one roof. You can involve the children in choosing which services to include in their health centre. It is a good area to set up when looking at topics such as Health, Growth and Ourselves.

What you will need

Reception desk, phone, diary, record cards

Waiting room, chairs, magazines, toys

Doctor's surgery - white coats (short-sleeved white shirts), nurse's uniform, doctor's kit, prescription pad, phone, medicine bottles, bandages.

Dentist's – white coats, mask, gloves, plastic bib or apron for patient, special chair (a swivel office chair works well), mirror, posters of teeth and dental hygiene, charts, penlight or small torch, toothbrushes, toothpaste, pink/green drink, tissues, stickers for brave children.

Optician's – special chair (see above), mirror, torch, eye chart with letters and colours, lots of glasses (frames only), brochures about glasses/contact lenses.

Baby clinic – nurse's uniform/apron, baby dolls, clothes, equipment (bath, towels, powder, cream, wipes, nappies, dummy, food, bottles, buggy, toys, pram, blankets), weighing scales, record cards, weight charts, teapot and cups and saucers.

Things to make and do

Ask each child to write their name on a small record card for the health centre reception desk.

Draw round a child on a large piece of paper and use as a poster for the doctor's surgery. Label the parts of the body. Try painting a skeleton using white paint on black sugar paper.

Make eye charts using letters, lower case and capital, shapes and colours for the optician's.

Setting up

Start by setting up the doctor's surgery and waiting room with comfortable chairs, magazines and toys.

Add a reception area with a desk, chair, phone and appointment diary. Put the record cards in alphabetical order into a small box file.

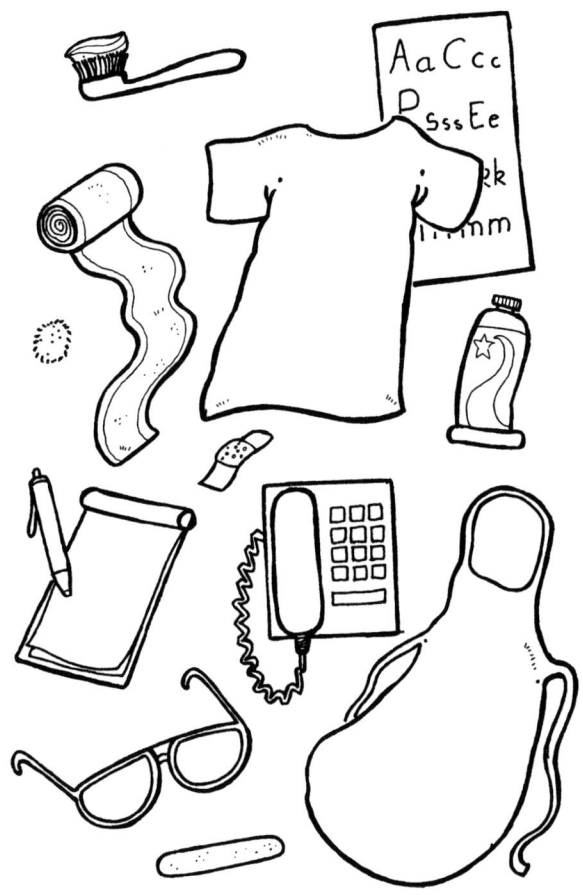

Add other rooms/surgeries one by one so that children have a chance to appreciate differences in roles and get the most out of each area.

Starting off

Talk to children about their local health centre. What services does it provide? Look at photographs of dentists, doctors and opticians. Decide what to include in your health centre.

Read *Topsy and Tim at the Dentists/Doctor* by Jean and Gareth Adamson (Ladybird), *A Day in the Life of a Doctor/Dentist* (Franklin Watts) or *The Baby's Catalogue* by Janet and Alan Ahlberg (Puffin).

Safety Remind children that they should never take pills or medicines without their parent's knowledge. Do not let children put any tools or toothbrushes, other than their own, into their mouths. Don't shine lights into children's eyes at the optician's. Just pretend!

Roles Doctor, nurse, receptionist, patient, dentist, optician, mum, dad, baby.

Visits and visitors

Contact your local health education centre for further resources such as giant model teeth and toothbrush, skeleton, posters, and so on.

Invite any parents who work in any of the health services to visit and talk to the children about what they

Role Play

do. Ask them to bring in any resources the children could add to the role-play areas.

Visit your local baby clinic or ask a health visitor to come and talk to the children about being healthy.

Invite a new parent and baby to visit the setting. The children could watch the baby being bathed and talk about how to help with a baby at home.

Outside play
Design and build a play area for children visiting the health centre to play safely in. Put a selection of sit and ride toys outside for children to play with.

Home links
Invite parents to talk to their children about visiting different health professionals. Try to discourage the 'I hate the dentist' attitude!

Hold a 'Clean your teeth' day. Ask parents to send children in with their toothbrush in a named bag. All children can clean their teeth after snack time. You provide toothpaste. Talk about how to clean teeth effectively – up and down movement, remember all sides of your teeth, and so on.

Organise a 'Bring and buy toy sale' at the end of the topic. Ask children to bring in any toys, in good condition, that they have grown out of. Send proceeds to a local children's charity.

Personal, Social and Emotional Development
Talk about children's experiences visiting the doctor, dentist or optician. How did they feel before the visit? And after? (PS2, 3, 6)

Do the children know anyone who has poor sight or hearing? How could they help them use the health centre? Make a story tape for a partially sighted child. Learn some sign language. (PS1, 2, 4)

Talk about babies who are born premature and need special care. (PS4, 6)

Encourage children to share the special equipment, such as the doctor's kit, and to take turns at being the patients. (PS8)

Invite children to bring in photos of themselves as babies to put up on the wall of the clinic. Can they recognise each other from the photos? (PS1, 8)

Communication, Language and Literacy
How does the doctor find out what is wrong with the patient? 'Where does it hurt?' 'Can you move your hand like this?' (L1, 4, 6)

Take turns to chat in the waiting room, 'What time is your appointment?' 'Have you got a sore throat like me?' 'The doctor is running late!' (L 4, 5, 6, 7)

Use record cards in the baby clinic and note information on weight, injections and any illnesses. (L1, 4, 16)

Use appropriate language in role – 'Can I have an appointment please?' 'Those frames really suit you, madam.' 'Are your teeth hurting?' 'Open wide.' 'How old is your baby?' (L10)

Make clear signs and notices for the different departments. Put a sign on the doctor's door saying 'Surgery – open 9.00 to 12.00.' Put the doctor's or dentist's name on the doors. (L12, 16)

The receptionist can give out appointment cards with the patient's name and time and date of appointment written on it. (L16, 17)

Write prescriptions for medicines and pills - 'Take one pill, two times a day.' (L16, 17)

Make a baby name book with the children. Find out about meanings of different names. (L14, 17)

Mathematical Development
The doctor can use numbers – 'Breathe in. Cough three times. And once more.' 'How long have you been feeling ill?' (M1, 2, 6)

Help children to listen to their pulse or heartbeat and count. (M1, 2)

Count teeth. Compare numbers. Use record cards or charts with child's name to show number of teeth. (M1, 2, 3, 4)

Make an eye chart with shapes to count and numbers to read. (M1, 2, 3, 9)

'How many patients are in the waiting room?' 'I have already seen four.' (M1, 2, 4, 5)

'My prescription says take three tablets. I've taken two, now I only have to swallow one more.' (M1, 3, 4)

Make pretend medicines in the water tray using clear bottles and coloured water. Seal the bottles and use them in the doctor's surgery (see 'Safety'). (M11, 12)

Undress and weigh the babies and teddies at the baby clinic. Weigh the children and measure how tall they are to record on their cards. Be sensitive to children who may be overweight. (M3, 12)

Knowledge and Understanding of the World

Encourage children to think about using all their senses in the health centre: smell of disinfectant, sound of dentist's drill and babies crying, looking at eye chart, taste of dentist's drink and touch of a cuddly baby. (K1)

Find out about how our bodies, teeth and eyes work using non-fiction texts, CD-Roms and internet. (K2, 4)

Cook some apples until they soften into puree. Compare with raw apples. Talk about baby food and milk teeth. Taste some baby foods. Can children identify the flavours? (K1, 3, 4)

Talk about looking after teeth properly, regular brushing and not eating too many sweets. Make healthy snacks – chop up raw carrots, apples and other fresh fruit. (K1, 4, 6)

Look at the baby photos (see PSED). How have the children changed? What can they do now that they could not do when they were babies? (K3, 4, 8)

Use a computer to record all children's names for the health centre. What other technology does the optician or dentist use? (K7)

Talk about bumps, bruises, cuts, injuries and illnesses that children or their families have suffered. (K8)

Physical Development

How does it feel to move around without being able to see? Work in pairs with one partner blindfolded. Can the sighted partner guide their friend around the health centre? (PD1, 2, 3)

Try pushing a baby doll in a pushchair around equipment without bumping into things. (PD1, 2, 3)

Sing 'Heads, shoulders, knees and toes'. Try missing out some words and just touching the parts of the body. (PD2)

Talk about the importance of warming up before exercising. Play a follow my leader game to warm up different parts of the body. (PD2, 4, 5)

Try some target games using skittles, bats, and balls to test children's hand to eye coordination. (PD2, 60)

Creative Development

Look in a mirror and paint a self-portrait to hang on the health centre walls. (C1)

Make posters for the doctor's showing what we need to do/eat to keep healthy. (C1)

Paint giant mouths and stick shiny white paper teeth in them. How could they show rotten teeth? Display them on the dentist's walls. (C1)

Sing and act out 'Miss Polly had a dolly'. (C2)

Play a listening game at the doctor's to check hearing. Make sounds and patterns on instruments for children to identify and copy. (C2)

Be dramatic. Go into the dentist's, wailing and groaning with a terrible toothache. What can anyone do to help? (C4)

Make baby toys for the clinic. Use black and white paper to make patterns on small card circles. Suspend these from a metal clothes hanger to make a mobile. (C4)

Design and make some trendy glasses frames for Eyes 'R' Us, the new optician's. Cut out frames for the children to decorate outlandishly with sequins, pearly paint, feathers and glitter. (C5)

Role Play

Hospital

> Adapt to a vet's

One of the most popular role-play scenarios is the hospital. This fits in well with the theme of 'People who help us' and can also be useful if a child in the group has to attend hospital and is feeling apprehensive (see also pages 17-19, 'Health centre'). Then get value added play by transforming the hospital into a vet's.

What you will need

For dressing up – doctor's coats (short-sleeved white shirts), nurse's uniforms (blue dresses, aprons, hats, badges, watches), theatre gowns (short-sleeved green or blue shirts worn back to front), masks, patients' dressing gowns, pyjamas, slippers, cuddly toys

Beds – small camp bed, mattress, inflatable lilo, cots

Bedding – sheets, blankets, pillows, small duvets

Reception desk – phone, computer, diary

Signs for different wards and departments

Visitor's room – chairs, magazines

Hospital shop – get well cards, flowers

Clipboards/medical charts

Doctor's kit – stethoscope, syringe, blood pressure pump, scissors, tweezers, cotton wool

Forehead thermometer

Bandages, slings

Medicine bottles with child safety lids

X-ray machine

Operating table, screens

Child-sized wheelchair

Child-sized crutches

Next stop

Close the hospital. Ask children to bring in lots of soft toy animals (dogs, cats, rabbits and small pets) and open a vet's surgery.

Add carrying baskets, cages, weighing scales, animal food products, and leaflets about caring for animals.

Open a waiting room with chairs, magazines and tea/coffee making facilities.

Things to make and do

Make signs and notices for the different wards and departments (see 'Setting up').

Build an x-ray machine out of big boxes painted black. Stick a sheet of silver foil on one side. Position them so children have to stand in between them to have a picture taken.

Make an ambulance from a large piece of card. Cut out windows, paint white and add yellow/green stripes. Fix to two chairs for children to sit in and pretend to drive to emergencies.

Make pretend plaster casts to fit on broken arms and legs using Modroc. Shape around a plastic bottle and then slide off when dry so children can wear them.

Make small pets (mice, hamsters, gerbils) for the vet's from old grey/brown socks (stuffed with old tights); add buttons for eyes and a felt nose.

Setting up

Make as many beds as possible, both child-sized and doll-sized.

Decide about different wards or departments, for instance, x-ray, children's, broken limbs and infectious diseases.

Set up a reception desk with phone, computer screen, appointment diary, and a list of patients' names for the day.

Make an operating theatre with a high table, screens, lights and pretend tools!

Starting off

Use children's own experiences as a starting point. Not knowing what to expect can be a major source of fear.

Read *Going to the Hospital* or *The New Puppy* from Usborne First Experiences (Usborne) or *Mog and the Vee Eee Tee* by Judith Kerr (Collins).

Safety Emphasise careful use of the doctor's kit and all pieces of equipment. Discuss the dangers of real syringes, medicine and tablets. and make sure children understand that this is play equipment.

Roles Doctor, nurse, vet, patient, visitor, ambulance driver, paramedic.

Visits and visitors

Invite any parents who work in a hospital or vets to talk to the children about what they do. Warn them in advance if any children are expecting a visit to hospital soon so they can work with you to ease any apprehension.

Ambulance crews and paramedics are often willing to come along and talk to the children, demonstrating some of their equipment and techniques. Invite them to talk to the children about simple first aid and ways that even young children can help in an emergency.

Outside play

Set up an ambulance station outside (see 'Things to make and do'). Use a bike and helmet for the paramedic and add coloured warning strips and a doctor's bag.

Home links

Encourage parents to talk to children sensitively about their own experiences of hospital. What happened when they were born?

Ask families if they know anyone who is in hospital that the children could make get well cards for or write letters to.

Ask parents to join you for a keep fit session with their children.

Invite children and parents to bring pets into nursery to visit the vets. Ask them to find out some information about their pet so they can talk to the children. Has their pet ever had to visit the vet? Check if any children are afraid of animals or have allergies to fur.

Personal, Social and Emotional Development

Are the children worried or fearful of hospitals? Some may have felt pain, lost a relative or witnessed pain in someone else. This needs to be handled sensitively, and may involve talking to parents if appropriate. (PS4, 6)

Children's earliest experiences of death are often associated with pets. This will often be acted out at the vet's. Help children to talk about losing a special pet. *Read Goodbye Mog* by Judith Kerr (Collins). (PS4, 6)

Children can be encouraged to think about the feelings of others and so develop some empathy. 'I'm sorry you are feeling poorly.' 'Oh dear, is your cat ill?' (PS4, 9, 12)

Encourage children to share special equipment and take turns with different roles. Be careful that boys do not insist on always being the doctors and refuse to be nurses. Photos, television programmes and stories that challenge these assumptions are useful. (PS7, 8, 9)

Talk about hygiene and why it is important to keep everything clean in hospital. (PS10)

Putting doctor's coats and hospital gowns on will give the children opportunities to practise independence in dressing. (PS10)

Communication, Language and Literacy

Give children an opportunity to talk to the group about their own experiences of hospital. (L1, 4, 5, 6)

Make up rhymes for 'hospital' words, for example pill – bill, bed – head, pet – vet, cat - mat. Can the children collect and write some poems to make a book for the patients to read in hospital? (L3, 7)

How do you make a bed? Can they talk through the sequence of actions as though showing a new nurse how to do it? (L5)

Explore new vocabulary in the hospital environment – emergency, accident, operation, injection, stitches, medicine, paramedic, x-ray, and parts of the body. (L8)

Ask children to talk to each other in a caring way. They will use gestures, intonation of voice and facial expressions to show meaning to the listener. 'Can you tell me your name and address?' 'Where does it hurt?' 'Are you not feeling any better?' (L10)

Make a hospital alphabet chart to put on the wall: a – ambulance, b – bed, c – cold, d – doctor, and so on. (L12)

Place clipboards at the end of each bed with the patient's name on. The doctor can make notes about progress or treatment on the chart. (L16, 17)

Children can make name badges – Doctor Lucy, Nurse Adam. (L17)

Role Play

Mathematical Development

Count toes, fingers, ribs, eyes, spots. (M1, 2)

Encourage children to use numbers in their role play. 'This prescription says take one pill, four times a day.' 'To call the ambulance you must dial 999.' (M1, 2, 3)

'You need two spoonfuls of medicine. Open wide. Well done! One more!' (M1, 2, 4)

Compare sizes. 'This bandage is longer than that one.' 'Pass me the big bottle of medicine.' (M9)

Use numbers to solve time problems. 'Your operation is not until 3 o'clock. It's 1 o'clock now. You will have to wait two hours.' (M1, 7, 11)

Put away the doctor's kit, matching the equipment to the shapes in the case. (M9, 10)

Knowledge and Understanding of the World

Encourage children to look at similarities and differences between themselves and others: hair, eyes, skin and size. Compare fingerprints. Make charts for the hospital wall showing their results. (K1, 2, 3)

Talk about and act out the pattern and routine of a day in hospital for the doctor or nurse, and the patient – waiting for a visit, meals, treatment, sleep. (K2, 3)

Use a forehead thermometer strip to take a patient's temperature. (K1, 4)

Invite children to investigate how our bodies work. Ask them to feel their pulse or heartbeat, and then jump up and down 30 times and feel it again. What happens? (K4)

Look at the use of technology in hospitals. Put children's names on a computer screen. Talk about x-ray machines and monitors that read heartbeats. (K7)

Use a photocopier to take images of hands and feet to use as pretend x-rays. (K7)

Give children opportunities to talk to the group about their own experiences of hospital. (K8)

Use non-fiction texts to find out about caring for animals. Cut, stick and write leaflets for the vet's. (K2, 7, 9)

Physical Development

How will they carry the poorly dolls and animals to the hospital? (PD1, 2)

Find out about how bodies move, and what happens when some joints don't work. Practise walking to the hospital with a knee that won't bend or a sore arm. (PD2)

Talk about keeping fit and taking regular exercise. Organise a keep fit class for children with simple warm-up exercises and movements to rhythmic music. Use hoops, ribbons and balls to vary activity (see 'Home links'). (PD4, 5, 6)

Borrow a set of small crutches from your local hospital and let children take turns using them to move around the room. (PD2, 6, 7)

Have fun putting bandages and slings on each others arms, legs, hands, feet and heads. (PD8)

Creative Development

Make x-ray pictures using white straws on black sugar paper. Hang them up in the operating theatre. (C1)

Paint funny pictures for the children's ward to cheer up the sick children. (C1)

Sing and act out 'My poorly pet needs to see the vet (three times), He/she has hurt his/her leg/tail/ear', and so on. (Tune: 'Skip to my Lou') (C2)

Choose recorded music to play in the hospital to soothe the listeners. (C3)

Be dramatic. A patient won't stay in bed/eat any food/take any medicine. What will the doctor or nurse do? (C4)

Design and make get well cards for the hospital shop or to send to someone in hospital (see 'Home links'). (C5)

Police station

Adapt to a fire station

Children instinctively enjoy playing games that involve rescuing or chasing and catching each other. Hopefully, a police station will not be within their immediate experience but a visit from a friendly officer can set the scene for some imaginative role play, fun and mayhem. You will need to set up a home corner alongside the station so the burglars have somewhere to burgle! This is a good area to open with the themes 'People who help us' and 'Work'.

What you will need

For dressing up – uniforms, cut-down jackets or tabards from educational suppliers, shirts, ties, waistcoats, helmets, boots

Whistles, handcuffs

Telephone, diary

Computer

Notepads

Radios

Desk and chairs

Tape recorder

Fingerprint equipment

Camera (Polaroid if possible)

Clock

Jail cell, keys

Police car, bike

Cones, stripy tape

General home corner equipment

Things to make and do

Make a large cut-out police car or fire engine shape from thick cardboard or paint onto a screen. Secure to the sides of two chairs.

Adapt sit and ride toys by adding blue lights and stripes.

Setting up

Use the bars from a cot or stair gate to create the bars in a jail cell, placed between screens or boxes.

Set up a front desk. Use a high table or screen with a window. Add telephone, diary and computer.

Make an interview room with table, chairs and tape recorder. Put up 'Wanted' posters (see Creative Development).

Put up signs: Police, Fire, Entrance, Private, Interview room, Exit.

Next stop

Adapt to a fire station. Add yellow helmets, breathing masks, trousers, gloves and boots to dressing-up clothes.

Change the police car into a fire engine.

Provide ladders, garden hose, buckets, alarm bell and fireman's pole to slide down.

Starting off

The best way to start is with a visit from a professional (see 'Visits and visitors').

Talk about the work of the emergency services. Make a list of all the jobs the police do to keep us safe. Have the children any first-hand experiences they can share with the group? Take care to be extra sensitive with this topic. Some children's experiences may have been traumatic or disturbing.

Role Play

Read *Topsy and Tim Meet the Police* by Jean and Gareth Adamson or *A Day in the Life of a Police Officer/Firefighter* (Franklin Watts). Talk sensitively to the children about stranger danger.

Safety Be sensible using the handcuffs. Don't be over enthusiastic about catching 'criminals'. Remind children that they are only pretending.

Roles Superintendent, detective, police officer, criminal, fire chief, fire fighter, house owner and families, car driver.

Visits and visitors

It may be possible to arrange a visit to the local police station or for an officer to visit your setting. Ask the police officer to bring uniforms, artefacts and even a patrol car to show the children. Take 'mug shots' using a Polaroid camera and fingerprints. Invent possible offences and punishments. Display photos in the police station.

Visit the local fire station or invite the fire service to send an engine to visit the nursery. The crew can explain their role, why they wear protective clothing and how the fire engine works.

Outside play

Set up a training assault course for the police and fire officers to use to keep fit. Use climbing and balancing equipment.

Make a road layout with road signs, traffic crossings, and police officers directing the sit and ride toys.

Use buckets of water and hoses to put out pretend fires.

Home links

Contact the local fire station to check if they have an open day.

Ask parents to look out for opportunities to look at fire engines, police cars and ambulances at fetes, public events and festivals.

Check with parents in case children have had any difficult experiences with the emergency services.

Personal, Social and Emotional Development

Encourage children to take turns at being the police officer and burglar. It is important to share the popular equipment such as handcuffs and fire hose. (PS1, 8, 11)

Invite children to talk to the group about 'A day in the life of a fire fighter or police officer'. (PS2, 3)

'My bike has been stolen.' How would the children feel if this happened to them? Which police officer is able to help? How does it feel to help someone else? (PS2, 4, 6)

Use lipstick or finger paint to make fingerprints on an identity card. Look at the different shapes and patterns and explain that they are all unique. (PS3, 4)

What happens if the traffic lights break down? How could the police officers help? (PS4, 8)

Talk to the children about fire, keeping safe, smoke alarms, fire extinguishers, and what to do if they see or smell smoke at home or school – tell an adult, phone the emergency services, dial 999. (PS4, 6)

Organise a fire drill and explain to the children how it is important to practise leaving the building quickly and quietly, just in case there was ever a real fire. (PS6, 7)

Encourage children to dress themselves in the uniforms and to help each other with buttons and fastenings. (PS4, 10)

Talk about the 'bad' things that some people do that get them into trouble with the police such as stealing and vandalising things. Help children to realise that they can role play stealing but that it is not the right thing to do in real life! (PS9, 12)

Communication, Language and Literacy

Read *Burglar Bill* by Allan Ahlberg (Puffin). Make up stories about burglars to role play in the home corner and police station. (L3, 9)

Ask children to talk to each other using police radios. 'I can see him walking near the garage.' 'Stop the red car. It's been stolen!' (L4, 7)

Police officers can use notebooks to make notes when they are talking to witnesses. 'Did you see anyone looking suspicious? What did she look like?' (L4, 16)

Invite children to take turns at being the boss or superintendent and tell others what to do. 'Chase that man!' 'Climb up and rescue the boy quickly!' (L5)

Ask children to interview each other. 'Where were you on Saturday night?' Tape record their conversations. (L6, 7)

Practise speaking on the telephone. Phone the police or fire service. 'My house is on fire.' 'What is your address, sir?' (L10)

Listen to police call signs that use names to represent initial letter sounds in registration numbers, for example Alpha is A, Bravo is B. (L12)

Help children to look at words and pictures in safety leaflets from the police and fire services. (L13, 14)

Children can make name badges for themselves: Constable Tom, Sergeant Sue. (L17)

Mathematical Development

Make number plates for the sit and ride toys. Look at some real ones. How many letters and numbers do they use? Help children to design their own – JOE 5. These can be noted down by the police officers! (M1, 2, 3)

Help children to add numbers to their name badges, for example PC0341. (M1, 3)

Talk about time. How many minutes will it take the police or fire service to get to the house? How long has the fire been burning? When did the burglar escape? (M1, 11)

Talk about speed limits. Make speed signs of 10, 20 and 30 mile per hour limits. Draw speed camera signs. (M1, 3, 4)

Arrange an identity parade. Number the children and ask the witness to say which number they think committed the crime. (M1, 3, 10)

Look at stripes and patterns on police cars and warning signs. Ask children to design their own bright patterns to put on police cars. (M8)

Use everyday words to describe position. 'He's run behind the garage.' 'I'll get you down. Climb down the ladder.' (M10)

Knowledge and Understanding of the World

Make a telephone using two plastic cups or yoghurt pots and a length of string. Pull the string taut and ask two children to send a message to each other across the room. (K1, 4, 5)

Use magnifying glasses to examine clues, fingerprints and scratches left by the burglar. (K1, 3, 9)

Investigate fingerprints. Press sticky fingers on glass or clear plastic, dust with fine talcum powder and see the fingerprints appear. Do they match the fingerprints on the identity card? (see PSED) Enlarge fingerprints using a photocopier. (K2, 4, 7)

Make walkie-talkie radios using small boxes, blue/black paint, PVA glue, straws and buttons. (K5, 6)

Make a set of traffic lights using red, orange and green circles to use to direct the traffic. (K5, 6, 9)

Physical Development

Have a safe car chase using the sit and ride toys. Make sure children know how to stop safely. Talk about speed limits and cameras. (PD1, 2, 3)

Practise climbing ladders on the climbing frame and sliding down poles. (PD2)

Firefighters have to carry heavy weights. Practise carrying big dolls or teddies and giving them 'fireman's lifts'. (PD1, 2)

Emergency service personnel need to be fit. Go round the assault course (see 'Outside play') or the indoor climbing equipment. What happens to your body as you exercise? (PD4, 5)

Use cones and tape to cordon off an area for the children to move around on foot or sit and ride toys. Ask the police officers to direct the traffic safely. (PD2, 3, 6)

Creative Development

Design posters about fire safety for the fire station. (C1)

Paint portraits of burglars or criminals to make 'Wanted' posters for the police station. (C1)

Draw identikit pictures of criminals using stick-on face shapes, hair, eyes, nose, mouth and any distinguishing features. Does it look like anyone they know? (C1)

Draw round two children and make them into collages of police officers. Write down all the jobs the police do in speech bubbles around the figures and display on the wall of the police station. (C1, 5)

Sing 'London's burning'. (C2)

Be dramatic. Come into the police station and give yourself up, confessing to stealing something special. Let the children put you in jail. (C4)

Garage

Role Play

It's important to encourage a non-gender stereotyped approach to all role-play areas especially those with a traditional male or female environment. Open a garage in your setting and encourage the children to take on roles that they may have assumed were not for them. Relate this to the theme of Journeys, Travel or Transport.

What you will need

For dressing up – overalls, old short-sleeved adult shirts, baggy trousers

Selection of sit and ride toys – cars, bikes, scooters, tricycles

Toolboxes

Tools (real and plastic) – spanners, hammers, pliers

Radio

Petrol pumps (see 'Things to make and do')

Shop or payment kiosk – cash till, money, credit cards, snacks, sweets, newspapers, magazines, buckets of flowers

Reception area – telephone, diary

Car wash – buckets, hose, watering cans, sponges, brushes, shammy leathers, cloths, empty bottles of car shampoo and polish

Next stop

Open a driving test centre. Use L-plates and make driving licences.

Make a road layout with road signs, crossing signals and traffic lights. Talk about road safety and crossing the road.

Things to make and do

Make a petrol pump by painting a large rectangular cardboard box and attach a piece of tubing for the hose. Attach two old CDs as dials and add numbers to show amounts of money or fuel.

Make tissue paper flowers for the garage shop.

Collect empty crisp packets. Fill with scrunched-up newspaper and seal securely.

Construct a car ramp and low platform using Quadro or similar big construction toy, so children can lie under cars when working as a mechanic.

Write price labels for new vehicles. Use bigger amounts such as £1,000 and £2,000.

Setting up

Set up a reception or payment area with telephone, diary to take bookings for services and repairs, cash till, snacks, flowers and newspapers.

Arrange petrol pumps in a line. Park some sit and ride toys on the forecourt and add price labels. Chalk car park spaces on the floor so children can practise parking carefully inside the parking bays.

Starting off

Try to organise a visit.

Talk about children's experiences of a garage – buying petrol with parents, pumping up tyres, driving through the car wash, buying a new car.

Read *Mr Gumpy's Motorcar* by John Burningham (Jonathan Cape) or *Ben's Big Book of Cars* by Ben Blathwayt (Red Fox).

Safety Take care when using real tools. Ride sit and ride toys carefully at all times.

Roles Manager, mechanic, receptionist, petrol pump attendant, car salesperson, customer.

Visits and visitors

Walk in small groups to a nearby garage or petrol station. Make a list or draw a plan of which services it provides – air, water, petrol, snacks, new cars, repairs. Ask for examples of forms, leaflets and posters.

Invite a mechanic, garage worker, or keen parent to come and talk to the children about looking after a car.

Invite a road safety officer or school crossing patrol person to come in and talk to the children about how to keep safe when crossing the road.

Outside play

Set up a carwash with sponges, brushes, cloths, buckets of water and hoses and encourage children to clean the sit and ride cars. Cut a coin slot into a shoe box and use as the car wash token machine.

Choose one vehicle to be the breakdown truck. Equip it with a tow rope and brightly coloured sign. Go out and rescue broken down cars and tow them back to the garage.

Open a car hire business. Have a selection of bikes and

sit and ride vehicles for hire. Use tickets, money, and time how long children can borrow them for.

Home links

Ask parents to try to take children with them to the garage to buy petrol or use the car wash.

Encourage children to help wash the car at home.

Organise a 'Car wash day' when parents and teachers can have their cars washed at school for a small donation to school funds.

Personal, Social and Emotional Development

Operating the petrol pump and the role of mechanic with overalls and tools will be popular. Talk about sharing equipment and taking turns with different roles so that it is fair. (PS1, 8)

What happens when your car breaks down on a journey? Can anybody at the garage help? How does it feel when you can't get to where you were going? (PS4, 6)

Children need to work together to clean and repair the cars. They may need to ask each other for help to lift or carry heavy items. (PS8)

Children enjoy putting on overalls and getting dirty. They need to wash hands carefully afterwards. (PS10)

Give children the responsibility for tidying up the garage each day. Don't leave tools lying around. What could happen if someone left a spanner on the floor or didn't clean up a slippery patch of oil? (PS11, 12)

Communication, Language and Literacy

Children will interact with each other – 'What seems to be the problem?' 'My car won't start. It's making a funny noise.' (L4, 7)

Children can help customers by talking them through the sequence of events needed to fill up with petrol or use the car wash. (L5)

Extend vocabulary by introducing more technical words – engine, battery, plugs, tyres, wheels, carburettor, radiator, wipers, service, repair. (L8)

Put up signs at the garage – petrol, water, air, car wash, open, closed, pay here. (L13, 17)

Look at the motoring section of your local paper, magazines, adverts for cars, catalogues and car manuals. Design and write a leaflet for the garage, listing services and advertising new cars. (L14, 16)

Write a letter to the garage complaining about the noise and disturbance to neighbours. How will the children respond? Help them to write replies and think of arguments to keep the garage open. (L1, 7, 16)

Encourage children to phone and book their car in for a service or repair. Use a diary and record their names, date and time of appointment. (L17)

Role Play

Mathematical Development

Use real money in the garage shop and count change. (M1, 2)

Make number plates for the sit and ride toys using children's initials and numbers. (M1, 3)

Encourage children to count cars, wheels, money, and so on. 'Which car has got the most wheels?' (M2, 11)

Use numbers on petrol pumps - 'I have spent ten pounds'. (M3)

Enjoy using much bigger numbers when making price signs for the new cars (see 'Things to make and do'). (M3, 11)

Use invoice books to write out bills and receipts, and collect payment. (M3, 4, 11)

Children can use language to measure amounts such as more, less, full, empty, heavier, lighter. 'How many litres of petrol do you want?' 'Two more litres, please.' (M4, 12)

'Where is the scooter?' 'It's behind the red bike.' (M10)

Knowledge and Understanding of the World

Talk about children's cars – colour, size, name, number of wheels and doors. Some children are fascinated by intricate details such as the shape of lights or indicators. Use this knowledge in the garage to describe cars. (K1, 2, 3)

Ask children to find out how cars work by looking at non-fiction texts and talking to adults. (K4)

Use large construction toys to build a car. Parts can then be taken off for other children to try and pretend to fix. 'Can you fix this wheel back on?' (K5, 6)

Make model cars from pre-cut soft wood, nails, cardboard, bottle tops, and so on. Display in the garage. (K5, 6)

Garages use computers to help diagnose problems with cars. Children could use a lead and plug the car engine into a pretend computer. (K7)

Has anyone's family bought a new car recently? What can they remember about the experience to share with the other children? (K8)

Look at pictures and models of old-fashioned, classic and vintage cars and bikes. How were they different from now? (K8)

Work in pairs to draw a plan of the garage with all the different areas. What do you like or dislike about the garage? (K9, 11)

Physical Development

Take care lifting and carrying heavy items at the garage. (PD1, 2)

Bring in some old tyres and ask children to work together to try rolling them around an obstacle course outside. (PD1, 2, 3)

Negotiate moving around on sit and ride toys without knocking into anything or anyone. Travel at different speeds around the equipment. Talk about safety and speed limits. (PD1, 2, 3)

Practise parking at the garage (see 'Outside play'). (PD3)

Use controlled movement and co-ordination to wash, clean and polish cars at the car wash. (PD6)

Children enjoy using tools. Let them handle safe mechanical equipment and with supervision use some real tools such as spanners, screwdrivers and pliers. (PD8)

Creative Development

Paint a giant mural of cars and other vehicles to display on the garage wall. (C1)

Sing 'My little car has broken down, broken down, broken down. My little car has broken down, it won't go'. (Tune: 'London Bridge'). (C2)

Read *Mr Little's Noisy Car* by Richard Fowler (Egmont). Talk about the sound effects you might hear in the garage. Create a garage soundscape. Use vocal, body and instrument sounds to make car noises, tools and machines. (C2)

Design and paint posters or adverts for new cars to hang up at the garage. What will the new car look like and what will it be called? (C4)

Be dramatic. Pretend to be an anxious customer whose car has broken down and is late for an important meeting. 'I will lose my job if I'm late!' How will the garage help? (C5)

Design a poster advertising free gifts when you buy £10 of petrol. What will the free gifts be? (C5)

Railway station

> **Adapt to an airport**

Children enjoy playing with trains and planes and making pretend journeys. Take this one stage further by creating a railway station or airport in your role-play area with opportunities for everyone to travel home, to the seaside and on holiday abroad. This could be part of a topic on Journeys, Holidays or Transport.

What you will need

For dressing up – jackets (shorten sleeves on adult jackets from charity shops), short-sleeved shirts, ties, hats, whistles, bags

Costumes for passengers

Train timetables and leaflets

Flag for guard

Hole punch for ticket collector

Luggage – suitcases, bags, rucksacks, trolley

Calculator

Cash till/money

Tickets

White or blackboard for emergency notices

Newsagent kiosk – comics, newspapers, magazines

Clocks – digital and analogue

Travel agents – desk, chairs, computer screen

Travel brochures, leaflets, posters

Telephones, paper, pencils

Foreign currency

Globe/atlas

Next stop

Adapt to an airport. Change train carriage to airplane.

Add customs and passport control. Make an x-ray machine for hand luggage.

Make a conveyor belt for baggage reclaim area.

Make a set of flight meals on small trays.

Things to make and do

Make notices in dual languages if possible – exit, entrance, trains, ticket office, waiting room, toilets, lost property. Use symbols and words.

Make an arrivals and departures board. Use a computer to print and enlarge names of local and faraway places.

Design and draw tickets and then photocopy them.

Make an aircraft control panel using an old box and black paint. Stick on round dials, reels, CDs, red and green lids for lights and buttons.

Setting up

Arrange chairs in pairs to make the train carriage or plane seats.

Build a driver's cabin or cockpit using special chairs and the control panel. Hang a uniform up for the driver or pilot to wear.

Set up a ticket office using a screen or large piece of card with a window cut in it. Use the cash till and issue tickets.

Starting off

Talk about children's experiences on trains and planes.
Read *A Day in the Life of a Train Driver* (Franklin Watts), *Topsy and Tim go on an Aeroplane* by Jean and Gareth Adamson (Ladybird) or some *Thomas the Tank Engine* stories.

Open the station or airport with an imaginary maiden trip to London or somewhere nearby that interests the children. Narrate what you would expect to see on the journey and when you arrive at your destination.

Safety Agree on how many children can safely sit on the train.

Roles Driver/pilot, stationmaster, guard, ticket seller, passenger, porter, air steward, travel agents.

Visits and visitors
Take children to a local railway or bus station to watch comings and goings of passengers and employees. Take a tape recorder and record some of the sounds – trains, doors opening, passengers, announcements, whistles blowing.

Invite any adults who work with trains or planes, or who have a special interest, to come and talk to the children.

Invite parents to come and talk to the children about other countries they have visited.

Outside play
Draw parallel train tracks on the ground with white chalk. Children can make trains in groups of three or four, holding round each other's waists. Adapt this to a runway using coloured chalks for the lights. Can children stop the plane before the lights run out?

Open a taxi rank at the station. Make a taxi from two chairs and a large piece of card cut into a car shape and painted black.

Home links
Make a collection of postcards from friends and family on holiday. Ask them to send pictures of trains and planes. Children can design a postcard showing their school to send to friends. Print copies of some of the designs and sell to raise funds.

Ask parents to save train tickets for children to copy and use at the station.

Choose a country and invite parents and children to 'Come on a day trip to _____'. Use the station or airport to get there. Dress up in costume, try new food, and listen to language, music, stories and customs.

Personal, Social and Emotional Development
Before visiting the station, talk about all the different people you are likely to see. Ask children to suggest appropriate ways of greeting people. Who is confident enough to talk to the stationmaster? (PS1, 2, 7)

Encourage children to share equipment and take turns with different roles. If driving the train is popular, try introducing shifts so that everyone can have a turn. (PS1, 8)

What happens if the train is late leaving or arriving? Who will have to explain to the passengers? Talk about how it feels to arrive late for something. (PS2, 4, 6)

Can all the children get on the train? What happens when it is full? 'Let the old lady sit down. You can stand up.' 'Is it possible for a wheelchair to go on this train?' (PS4, 8, 9)

Talk about different countries children come from or have visited to widen understanding of a variety of cultures. Look at a globe or atlas to find these countries. (PS5, 13)

Encourage children to be independent in choosing appropriate dressing-up clothes and dressing themselves. (PS10, 11)

Communication, Language and Literacy

Children can listen to sounds and announcements at the station and use them in their play. 'The train arriving at platform four is going to Birmingham.'

Invite children to take turns at being the stationmaster. 'You are selling tickets, you can be guard and you are the driver.' (L4, 5)

Use language to help solve problems. 'How can I get my pram on the train?' (L7)

Write out tickets with different destinations. 'I'm going to Glasgow to see my gran.'(L8, 16)

Ask children to find letter sounds in labels and signs at the station. (L12)

Make passports to use at the airport with self-portrait, information about child and signature. (L16, 17)

Write a list of what you need to pack in your suitcase. (L16)

Reserve seats using name labels. (L17)

Mathematical Development

Count the number of seats on the train. Number the seats with tactile numbers and write numbers on tickets. 'Can you find seat number three?' (M1, 2, 3)

How many people are in the queue? 'Let this gentleman go in front of you. He needs to sit down.' (M1, 2)

'There are six seats on the train. There are five of us. Will there be enough seats?' (M2, 5, 6)

Encourage children to use train timetables, clocks and arrival/departure boards in their conversations. 'My train leaves from platform one at 2 o'clock.' 'How long does it take to get to Bristol?' (M3, 11)

Create a pattern collage to guide unsighted passengers around the station. Use round bottle tops and small boxes stuck in a pattern on a strip of card. (M8)

'Put the big suitcase behind the seat.' (M10)

Use money to buy and sell train tickets. (M11)

Use bathroom scales to weigh suitcases. 'My bag is the heaviest.' (M12)

Knowledge and Understanding of the World

Station guards use flags and whistles to signal that a train is leaving. Talk about using different senses to send and receive signals. (K1, 4)

After visiting the station, talk about what children heard, saw, smelled, and touched. What did they like and dislike about the station? (K1, 9, 11)

'How will I get all my luggage on the train?' How could the station staff help? (K4, 5)

Discuss and re-enact journeys that children have made. Where were they going and why? (K4, 8)

Make a megaphone from a semi-circle of card to announce train departures. 'Stand clear of the doors, please.' (K5, 6)

Look at how wheels work. Build model trains/planes using construction toys, junk, and wood with wheels, cogs and axles. (K5, 6)

Look at how technology is used in travel, such as computers, internet, ticket machines, air traffic control, and so on. (K7)

Physical Development

Children have to carry heavy luggage carefully. (PD1, 2)

'The train is leaving in two minutes. Can you get to the station in time?' (PD1, 2, 3)

Use two coloured flags or discs to direct the plane to land safely on the runway. (PD1, 2, 6)

Can children travel around the equipment in different ways? (backwards, forwards, fast, slow) (PD5, 6, 7)

Operating dials, steering wheels and levers to drive the train require manipulative control. (PD6, 8)

Use sit and ride toys as trains and have a race. (PD6)

Creative Development

Paint posters to advertise journeys on trains/planes to different countries. (C1)

Sit on the train and make up train sounds and rhythms: diddle-ee-dum, diddle-ee-dum. (C2)

Sing 'My blue train is standing in the yard, chuff (twice), My blue train is standing in the yard, but now it's time to leave, Faster, faster, faster, faster (three times), And now it's time to stop!' (Tune: 'John Brown's body') (C2)

Be dramatic. The message board says 'The 10 o'clock train to London is cancelled'. How will the passengers react? What will the stationmaster say? (C4)

Choose suitable background music for the station. Will the children choose soothing classical music or loud rock music? (C4)

Design new trains and make group collages to hang on the station walls. (C5)

Role Play

Supermarket

One of the earliest experiences of the outside world for many young children is a visit to the local supermarket with their parents to do the weekly shop. Some children will already have begun enjoying role play at home by setting up a shop and practising buying and selling. Use this as a starting point for creating a food shop or supermarket in your role-play area. It could be part of a topic on Food, Health, Ourselves, Senses, Work or People who help us.

What you will need

For dressing up - uniforms

General – purses, baskets, trolley, leaflets, posters, ingredients for cooking

Check-out – cash till, money (real and plastic), bags, conveyor belt, chair

Grocery – shelves or bookcase, different sized and shaped food boxes (lots of variety including vegetarian food and food from a variety of cultures), empty plastic bottles, tins

Bakery – plastic and salt dough cakes, biscuits and bread, trays, paper bags, tongs, cake boxes

Vegetables – plastic and real vegetables, weighing scales, fruit trays and boxes

Things to make and do

Stuff empty food boxes, sliced bread bags and crisp packets with newspaper and tape up securely.

Make strings of sausages from old tights stuffed with more old tights!

Cut cakes out of blocks of sponge foam.

Make salt dough cakes, biscuits, jam tarts and ring doughnuts.

Fill individual silver foil trays with scrunched-up paper to make pies.

Make fruit and vegetables from scrunched-up newspaper, Modroc and paint.

Make signs for the different departments and/or posters illustrating what is on sale. Use cut-up magazines and children's own artwork.

Sew purses for children to use from felt, thread and Velcro.

Phone the council and arrange for a bottle bank to be positioned outside nursery/school for a week during the topic.

Setting up

You may decide to set up all the different departments together at the beginning or introduce them one by one.

Set up the check-out area first with the cash till, chair and low table. Put a large loop of black sugar paper along the length of the table so it can move like a conveyor belt.

Ask children to help stack the shelves or tables with food boxes. Put up posters, labels and prices.

Starting off

Choose a day to open the supermarket for the first time. Invite a parent, staff member or a minor celebrity to open it for you with a bit of a ceremony, cutting a ribbon and making a speech!

Read *Lucy and Tom's 123* by Shirley Hughes (Puffin) or *Going Shopping* by Sarah Garland (Puffin). (L3)

Safety Ask children not to open the food boxes as whatever it says on the outside they only have newspaper in them! Remind them to handle the equipment carefully.

Roles Manager, check-out operator, shop assistant, shelf stacker, baker, customer, security guard.

Visits and visitors

Organise visit/s to local supermarket. Look at the different departments and, if possible, behind the scenes at the bakery and warehouses (see Knowledge and Understanding of the World).

Before the visit, write a shopping list of ingredients for a recipe and buy them. Refer to the list at the shop, buy what's on the list, make the food and enjoy.

Invite parents/carers who work in a supermarket to visit and talk to the children about their work. Encourage children to think of questions they would like to ask.

Visit an open-air market in your local town. What do the different stalls sell?

Outside play

Open a market stall outside on a fine day.

Make a bottle bank out of a large box painted green with different-sized holes cut in it for children to post empty plastic bottles inside.

Organise a trolley dash outside using child-sized trolleys.

Home links

Ask parents to collect empty food packets and boxes, and labels from tins.

Invite parents to talk to their children about recycling and visit their nearest bottle bank.

With parents' help, open the bakery shop to sell homemade cakes as a fund-raising exercise.

Personal, Social and Emotional Development

Encourage children to take responsibility for keeping the shop tidy and returning items they buy to the right place when they have finished playing (PS8, 9, 11, 12).

Encourage children to share equipment and take turns with different roles. If using the cash till is the most popular, try introducing shifts so that everyone can have a turn. Develop new roles such as an awkward customer or lazy worker. (PS1, 7, 8)

What would happen if a child got lost in the supermarket? Who could help? Have any of the children ever got lost when out shopping? (PS2, 4, 6)

'Why are there no apples left?' How does a customer feel when the shop runs out of something they want? What will the manager say? (PS4, 9)

Talk about the importance of personal hygiene when cooking and handling food. (PS10)

Include food from different countries in the shop so children widen their understanding of a variety of cultures. (PS5, 13)

Communication, Language and Literacy

Play 'I went to the supermarket and bought a …………'. (L1, 7)

Children could imagine their first day at work. They don't know how to use the till, and/or they see someone take something without paying. (L4)

Invite children to take turns at being the manager and leading a meeting to organise the staff. 'First, I would like you to ….. and then……..'. (L5)

'What do you need?' 'I need to buy some sausages, baked beans and bread rolls for tea.' Write shopping lists and till receipts. (L7, 16)

Children will use appropriate language according to their role. Remind shop assistants to speak clearly and be polite: 'Can I help you?' (L10)

Children can make name badges and use open/closed/exit signs in shop. (L13, 17)

Help children to look at words and pictures in printed leaflets and food packaging. (L12, 15)

Mathematical Development

Encourage children to count items on shelves, trays and in and out of baskets. (M1, 2)

Write shopping lists: 3 oranges, 4 bread rolls, 1 bottle of tomato sauce, 2 boxes of cereal. (M2, 3)

Use weighing scales. Which potato is heavier? Compare two baskets of shopping. Who has got more items? 'I've got more cakes than you.' (M4, 12)

'We need six apples. You've got three apples and I've got two. How many more do we need?' (M5, 6, 7)

Ask children to design a logo for the supermarket using patterns. Reproduce this on bags, signs and posters. (M8)

Encourage use of mathematical language. 'I need a bigger box of cornflakes, please.' 'Have you got another cylinder of crisps?' 'Put the boxes on the top shelf, behind the tins.' (M9, 10)

Write price labels using 1p, 2p, 5p, and 10p. Use real and plastic money. 'How much will three bananas cost?' (M11)

Knowledge and Understanding of the World

Encourage children to use all their senses when visiting the local supermarket: smell of fresh bread, sight and touch of fruit and vegetables, sounds of people and machines, and taste of food. Buy a fish and take it back to the nursery where the children can look at and touch it. Try cooking it. Enjoy the smell and taste. (K1)

Set up a stall in the supermarket area for children to try out food on special offer. Encourage them to try new tastes. Choose yellow food - bananas, lemons, peppers, and cheese or red food – apples, tomatoes, peppers, and grapes. Don't forget to check for any allergies. (K1, 3)

Make fresh bread, cakes or pizzas with the children to sell in the supermarket and eat at snack time. Look at how materials change when cooked. Which tools will they need? (K3, 4, 5)

Make simple cake boxes from folded card (see below - your local bakers or supermarket may have some). (K5, 6)

Open a salad bar for the day. Let children wash, peel, chop and mix salads using vegetables, fruit, pasta and rice. (K6)

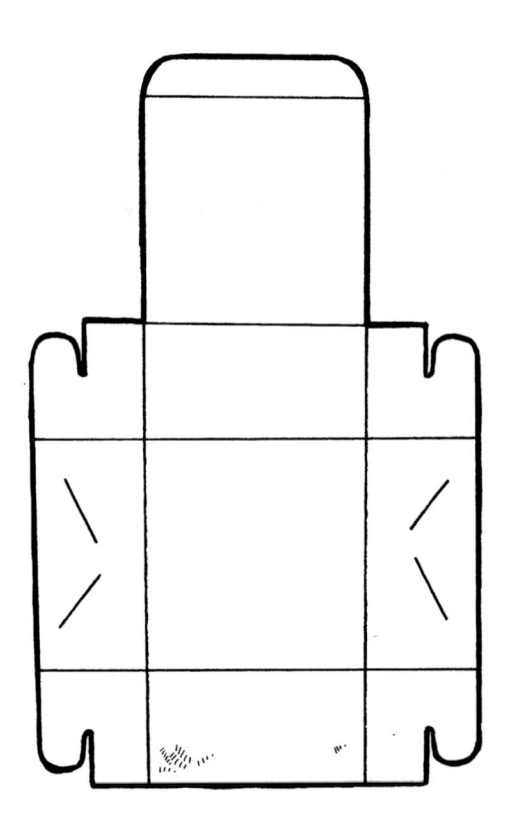

Use calculators to add up shopping. (K7)

Look at technology in supermarkets, such as the cash till, credit cards, bar codes, computer stock records. Why are these useful? Children could add bar codes to boxes and labels using thin and thick black lines. (K7)

What were shops like in the past? Ask grandparents to visit and talk about how shopping has changed. (K8)

Where does the food in shops come from? Trace the journey of milk or bread from field to shop. (K9)

Physical Development

It's important that children learn how to carry things carefully and safely – stacking boxes on shelves, sorting out more delicate items such as fruit, vegetables and cakes. (PD1, 2)

If the area is busy, children may need to say 'Excuse me' when squeezing past each other. (PD3)

Read *Oliver's Vegetables* by Vivian French (Hodder). Talk about eating healthy foods. How could you encourage children to buy healthy food at the shop? (PD4)

Pushing trolleys, carrying baskets, packing boxes, picking up fruit and making cakes all require different movements. (PD6)

Use sit and ride toys to take food to and from the shop. (PD7)

'Will this box balance on top of that one?' Build pyramids/towers with boxes to display goods in the shop. (PD6, 8)

Creative Development

Paint pictures or make collages of favourite food on paper plates to use as adverts in the shop. (C1)

Sing and act out 'Five currant buns in the baker's shop' and 'Ten big boxes standing on the shelf' ('Ten green bottles'). (C2)

Hold a 'Jelly day'. Vote on children's favourite flavour jelly. Buy, make and eat jelly. Sing 'Jelly on the plate'. Wobble like jellies. (C3)

Look at breakfast cereal boxes and ask children to design and make their own packaging for a new cereal to sell in the supermarket. (C4)

Be dramatic. Go into the supermarket and complain about a packet of broken biscuits, or mouldy fruit. 'These are all broken. I want my money back.' (C5)

Encourage children to share their experiences in the role-play area with the other children through talk and mime. (C5)

Shoe shop

> Adapt to a clothes shop or hat shop

All your children will have been to a shoe shop, experienced what it's like to have their feet measured, and gone through the process of buying new shoes. It can be a source of conflict, especially with older children. Possible themes include All about me, Clothes, Opposites and Growth.

What you will need

For dressing up – shoes of all shapes and sizes, sandals, slippers, boots, shoes from various countries, clown shoes, and so on

(Make sure you collect shoes that boys will enjoy trying on, too, such as men's shoes, boots and fancy trainers.)

A selection of general dressing-up clothes including multicultural outfits

Shoe boxes

Foot measures – borrowed or handmade

Bags

Jewellery

Cash till, money, credit card

Plastic carrier bags

Mirror

Comfortable chairs

Shelves and tables to display shoes

Shoe polish, cleaning equipment

Next stop
Open a clothes or hat shop.

Things to make and do
Ask your local shoe shop for lots of different-sized shoe boxes with lids. Try to borrow a child-sized foot measure.

Make a foot measure using a wooden ruler and a piece of card with two slits that can slide up and down to touch the foot.

Make an electronic foot measure. Draw outlines of a pair of feet on the inside base of a box. Add numbers. Children stand barefoot in the box. Slide a piece of dowelling down to touch the toes. You will have to provide the sound effects!

Make a machine to give out tickets with numbers on to organise turns.

Setting up
Set up a window display on a table using a selection of shoes and bags on different-sized stands. Cut out cardboard leg shapes to stick in the shoes and let children design crazy patterned tights and socks.

Arrange pairs of shoes on shelves for customers to browse. Provide a comfortable chair or two for customers to sit down.

Starting off
Read *Alfie's New Shoes* by Shirley Hughes (Red Fox). Talk about the experience of buying new shoes: queuing, waiting turns, taking shoes back, having feet measured, and choosing shoes.

Safety Don't climb on equipment wearing dressing-up clothes, big shoes and long necklaces.

Roles Manager, shop assistant, customer.

Visits and visitors
Take small groups to visit a local shoe shop or factory.

Visit a local museum to look at shoes through history.

Outside play
Organise a rainy day walk and ask children to bring in a pair of wellington boots to wear. Enjoy using umbrellas and jumping in puddles.

Draw lines with chalk on the outside area for children to parade in their new shoes. Try straight and wiggly lines, spirals, loops, and even a maze.

Home links
Ask parents to bring in pairs of unusual shoes, old, tiny and decorated shoes for the shop window display.

Encourage parents to show their children window displays in local shops.

Open a shoe shine service one day to raise funds. Charge parents 20 pence to have their shoes polished by the children, with staff help!

Personal, Social and Emotional Development

Encourage children to share the shoes and other equipment and take turns with different roles. If one particular pair of shoes is popular you may have to organise a timed turn. (PS1, 8)

Children can role play problem-solving in the shop: a customer who cannot find a shoe to fit; a naughty child who won't try on any shoes or one who doesn't like the pair their mum wants them to have. (PS2, 4, 6)

Invite children to take turns at being the manager, organising the other staff. What will they do if an assistant keeps arriving late for work and is lazy? (PS4, 7, 9)

Invite children to talk to the group about how to use the foot measuring tools. (PS2, 3)

Investigate any cultural traditions about shoes. Do you take your shoes off when you enter your house? (PS5)

Encourage the children to tidy up the shop at the end of each day. Put pairs of shoes together. Remember to return all the shoes to the shop when you have finished playing. (PS8, 9, 11)

Practise taking off and putting on shoes using different fastenings. Can the children show each other how to tie laces? (PS10)

What are the consequences of not getting new shoes when you need them? (PS12)

Communication, Language and Literacy

Learn the rhyme:

I can tie my laces, I can tie a bow,

I can do a buckle, I can use Velcro,

Putting on my new shoes, ready to go! (L2, 3)

Tell the story of 'The elves and the shoemaker'. Act out the story in the shoe shop. How will you show the difference between night and day? (L3, 4, 9)

Use the story of 'Cinderella' to talk about finding shoes that fit. (L3, 4, 9)

Children will use appropriate language so the sales assistants will be polite. 'Can I help you?' Customers could ask 'Have you got these red sandals in a size ten?' (L4, 10)

Make 'parking spaces' for shoes in the shop. Draw round the bottom of a pair of shoes and label them L – left and R – right. Park the shoes back there at the end of a busy day. (L5, 11)

Write an advert for a job in the shoe shop. Write applications and hold interviews. 'Why do you want to work in our shoe shop?' (L7, 16)

Write out orders and receipts for customers. (L16)

Make decorated boot pegs to keep wellington boots in pairs. Write names on the pegs. Children could take these home at the end of the topic. (L17)

Mathematical Development

Encourage lots of basic maths skills: sorting shoes into pairs, matching shapes, colours and sizes. (M1, 2, 3)

Count pairs of shoes and individual shoes. Count in twos. (M2)

Draw round a child's foot and cut out the shape. Use it as a non-standard measure in the shoe shop and outside. (M2, 9)

Measure the children's and adult's feet. 'What size shoe do I need?' Who has the smallest, biggest, longest and thinnest feet? (M3, 4, 9)

Organise a way of taking turns in the shoe shop using a ticket machine. Write numbers on the tickets and ask people to take one when they come in the shop. 'Who's got number nine?' (M3, 11)

Use real and pretend money. Put price labels on the shoe boxes. Which is the most expensive pair of shoes in the shop? Why? (M3, 4, 11)

'Are those shoes too small? Would you like to try a bigger size?' (M4, 9)

Knowledge and Understanding of the World

Encourage children to use all their senses in the shoe shop: the look of shiny new shoes, stiff feel of new shoes, smell of leather, and sound of tapping feet walking up and down the shop. (K1)

Talk about journeys on foot: walking to school, the park, shops and home. What have children noticed on their walk to school? (K2, 3)

Investigate how shoes are made. Which different materials are used? Where does leather come from? Look at old shoes and shoes from a variety of cultures. (K4, 8, 10)

Make sandals to sell in the shoe shop. Draw round both feet and cut them out of thin card. Fasten thin strips of bendy card or material across the top to slip the foot under. (K5, 6)

Use calculators to add up shopping. (K7)

Keep a list of customers' names and sizes on the computer. (K7)

Physical Development

It's important that children learn how to carry things carefully and safely – practise carrying shoe boxes around the shop. Stack the shelves sensibly. (PD1, 2)

Move around safely wearing shoes that don't fit! How will they move if the shoes are too small or belong to a clown? (PD1, 2)

Organise a 'Trainers day'. Ask all children to come to school wearing trainers and do lots of running, hopping, jumping and skipping. (PD2, 3, 4, 5)

Practise ball skills, dribbling and kicking at a target. (PD6)

Use polish, dusters and brushes to clean shoes in the shoe shop and at the shoe shine day (see 'Home links'). (PD6, 8)

Creative Development

Paint pictures of colourful shoes to hang in the shoe shop. (C1)

Print with bare feet and shoes with interesting soles on long rolls of lining paper. Use this to decorate the walls of the shoe shop. (C1)

Draw round your foot and design a shoe. Cut out the shape and cover in collage materials. Mount and display in the shop window. (C1)

Give old wellies or shoes a new lease of life by painting them with fluorescent and glitter paint. Sell them in the shoe shop. (C1)

Sing and act out: 'My new shoes are black and white, black and white, black and white, My new shoes are black and white, watch me walking'. (Tune: 'London Bridge'). Verses 2 - 4: 'fine and bright', 'quite a sight' and 'far too tight!' End the song by shouting 'Ouch!' (C2, 5)

Use shoes in the shop to make sounds: tapping, stamping, tip-toeing, leaping and running. (C2)

Be dramatic. Choose a special shoe to be a magic shoe. Ask children to imagine that this shoe can take them anywhere they want. Act out where they would like to go. (C5)

Role Play

Post office

The best play value can be gained from opening a post office with a sorting office behind the scenes, so children can find out more about how the service works. Most children will be familiar with the local post box, office and postman/woman and all seem to have a fascination for posting things. Combine this with a row or terrace of houses to extend the play. Themes to work with are: People who help us, Numbers and Journeys.

What you will need

For dressing up – uniforms (blue jackets, shirts, baggy shorts), hats

Large sacks, shoulder bags

Post box

Letters, envelopes, postcards

Writing paper, notelets, invitations, cards for different occasions

Pens, pencils, felt pens, crayons

Parcels, jiffy bags

Stamps, ink pad

Weighing scales

Sit and ride toys

Cash till, money

Forms

Old postage stamps, glue

Shoe boxes

Calendar

Next stop

Open a sorting office and operate a sorting machine (see 'Things to make and do').

Close the post office down due to lack of funds and a fall in the number of customers. What will the children choose to open in its place?

Things to make and do

Make an interesting collection of parcels, in different shapes and sizes, wrapped in plain brown paper, tied in string.

If you don't have a toy post box, make your own: cover and paint a large cardboard box bright red and cut a posting slot in one side. Remember to leave a hole at the back so the postman can empty it!

Make a red post van using a large piece of card cut into a van shape and painted red. Cut out a window and stick the van onto the side of a chair.

Tape or stick rows of shoe boxes together to make sorting shelves.

Build a conveyor belt or sorting machine. Make a loop of lining paper and fix it round a wooden slide or tabletop so that it is free to move. Packages will slide along as the belt is moved carefully (by hand of course!).

Setting up

Make the serving counter with a high table or a screen with a window. Try to have more than one so children have to use a queuing system.

Encourage the use of a writing area for children to write letters to post. Provide a good variety of writing materials.

Set up the sorting office behind a screen as a separate area.

Starting off

Read a selection of Postman Pat stories or *The Jolly Postman* by Janet and Allan Ahlberg to help the children think about the work of a postman or woman.

Walk to the nearest post box and post letters to the children (see 'Home links').

Safety Remind children not to unwrap the play parcels and to take care when carrying parcels not to fall over and hurt themselves or other children.

Roles Manager, counter staff, postman or woman, sorter, customer.

Visits and visitors

Ask your postman or woman to call and deliver the post in person to the children one morning. Help the children to prepare questions to ask in advance.

Take a small group of children to visit your local post office and make a list of all the services it provides. Collect some blank forms, leaflets and posters.

Outside play

Draw a wiggly route on the playground using chalk. Set the postman the task of riding his bike carefully along the track to each house. Position children along the route to receive mail.

Home links

Invite children to bring in a stamped addressed envelope from home with their own name and address or that of a relative. Help children to write a letter, seal it in the envelope and then walk to the nearest post box to post it. How many days does it take to arrive?

Ask parents to save old envelopes, stamps, parcels, packaging, and jiffy bags to bring in and be re-used in the post office.

Personal, Social and Emotional Development

Talk about how it feels to receive a letter or parcel through the post. Let children describe or bring in letters or cards they have received. (PS2, 4, 6)

Try out new roles – the forgetful postman, the angry customer. What happens if the postman gets lost or is always late? (PS1, 2, 9)

Bring in interesting shaped parcels to take to the post office. Can the children guess the contents? (PS1, 2, 7, 8)

Take it in turns to queue at the post office. How does it feel to be in the slow queue? What would an impatient customer say or do? (PS1, 8, 9)

Encourage children to take turns using the post van, and emptying the post box. If certain jobs prove popular, try introducing shifts. Who would like to work the night shift? (PS4, 7, 8)

Invite the children to choose which part of the post office they would like to work in and pick their own activity. (PS11)

Communication, Language and Literacy

Help children to learn their home address by heart. Can they address a letter to themselves? (L1, 5)

Make up stories and act them out: 'The lost letter' or 'A surprise invitation'. (L3, 4, 5)

Encourage children to use the days of the week. 'This letter will be delivered on Wednesday.' 'The parcel came yesterday, Monday.' Hang up a date chart or calendar so the children can change the date each day. (L5)

Invite children to read pretend letters to each other. 'This is from my gran. She says don't be late.' (L1, 4, 6)

Use appropriate language: 'Cashier number two, please.' 'Can you sign here and here, sir.' (L10)

Use stamp pads to frank and print forms. Make stamps of children's names using magnetic letters and wood blocks. (L4, 11, 17)

How many reasons can children think of to write a letter or send a card? Let children use different sorts and sizes of paper to write letters, make cards, pay bills and send postcards. (L16)

Mathematical Development

Count letters and parcels as they are collected from the post-box or as they move along the conveyor belt. (M1, 2)

Can the postman find the right house? 'This letter is for number eight and this one is for number seven.' Talk about odd and even numbers. (M1, 3)

'Put all the letters for number two in this box. How many are there? Are there more for number four?' (M1, 2, 3, 4)

'Pass me the small, square parcel, please.' 'Can you put the long, thin parcel in the bag?' (M9)

Measure parcels with rulers and tape measures. Will they fit through the letterbox? (M3, 11)

Use scales to weigh parcels. 'This is the heaviest one.' (M12)

Knowledge and Understanding of the World

Encourage children to use all their senses as they play: looking at parcels, reading addresses, touching packaging and bubble wrap, and scrunching crackly parcels. (K1)

Help the children to track the journey of a letter from writer to delivery. Use this to draw a poster to put up at the post office. (K2, 4, 9)

Work together to build the sorting machine. (K4, 5)

Use junk to make the other machines to use in the post office – scales, stamp machines, wrapping machines. (K5, 6)

Talk about emails, text messaging, faxes and new ways of communicating. Use the computer to help children send emails to parents or a friend. (K7)

Help children to draw maps to show the postman where to deliver the letters. (K9)

Physical Development

Children need to take care carrying heavy parcels and fragile packages. (PD1, 2)

Practise reaching letterboxes in different doors, stretching up high and bending down low. (PD2)

They may need to squeeze past people or things while carrying or delivering post. (PD3)

Take turns to give and follow directions to find the right house – four steps forward, turn left, three steps backwards, turn round, five steps forwards, turn right. (PD2, 3, 5)

Use sit and ride toys to deliver the post. (PD6, 7)

Wrapping parcels with paper and string, putting letters into envelopes, posting letters through post boxes all require increasing control. (PD6, 8)

Creative Development

Print wrapping paper using potato prints on white sugar paper. Try repeated patterns. (C1)

Print simple words using giant sponge letters and stencils. (C1)

Sing and act out: 'Five fat parcels in a postman's sack, All different sizes with a stamp on the back. Along comes the postman with his bag one day, Posts one letter and takes the rest away.' (C2)

Fill small boxes with dry rice, pulses, lentils, pasta, money, beads, sand. Wrap them up like parcels. When shaken, each will sound different. Can the children make some post office music? (C2)

Be dramatic. The postman drops all the letters in a puddle, or gets chased by a guard dog. What happens next? (C4)

Library

> Adapt to a museum, a bookshop or to include an art gallery

This area works best if children are able to enjoy the experience of visiting their school or local library and can understand the purpose, environment and atmosphere of a library. It fits in well with the themes of Books, People who help us, Stories and Opposites.

What you will need
General dressing-up clothes

Lots of books – fiction and non-fiction, all shapes and sizes

Shelves

Desk, telephone

Index cards

Tickets

Computer screen

Stamps, ink pad

Rug or carpet

Comfortable chairs

Beanbag seats and cushions

Magazines, newspapers

Book posters, catalogues

Tape recorder, headphones, story tapes

Next stop
Open an art gallery in the library. Mount and display children's artwork on walls in clip frames (see 'Home links').

Adapt into a museum of natural history, science or antiquities. Include a museum shop with postcards and gifts. Organise a dinosaur exhibition.

Turn the library into a bookshop.

Things to make and do
Cover a selection of books with sugar paper/plastic so that they are clearly library books, and put a sheet inside for the date stamp, attached with a paper clip.

Frame prints of famous works and hang on walls alongside children's artwork.

Make a CCTV camera for the art gallery using junk materials, cylinders and boxes, painted black.

Setting up
Display the library books on shelves.

Create a special comfortable reading area with beanbags and cushions for children to enjoy the books they have chosen. Include a listening corner with tape recorder, headphones and story tapes.

Set up a librarian's desk with computer screen. Attach a used pen to a piece of string for children to use as a pretend scanner. They will need to make the bleep sound as books are scanned in and out!

Use thick cord or rope to make a route around art exhibits. Secure to stands made from wooden broom handles stuck in plastic containers weighted with sand.

Starting off
After visiting your local library, explain to the children that you are setting up a role-play library so children can play with books and equipment. They will need to return the library books to the shelves each time they

have finished playing. Will you need to limit how many books each child can borrow?

Organise an opening event. Invite children to come dressed as a favourite book character for the day. Invite a local author or celebrity to come and open the library or museum.

Safety Handle books and exhibits carefully so they don't get damaged.

Roles Librarian, customer, museum guard, art critic, photographer.

Visits and visitors
Take children to visit the local library. Let them choose a book to take out, watch how the librarian issues it, and bring it back to share with others.

Invite the librarian to visit and talk to the children about books and working in a library: issuing and checking library tickets, choosing and cataloguing, returning books to shelves.

Visit your local art gallery or museum and talk about paintings and exhibits.

Invite a local painter or sculptor to come and work with the children.

Outside play
Find an outside wall that the children can paint with emulsion paint and create a mural. Draw simple geometric patterns, numbers or an animal design. Use bold colours.

Home links
Ask parents to take their children to join the local library.

Ask parents to bring in books their children have finished with and sell them on a second-hand bookstall to raise funds.

Invite parents to come in at the beginning and end of each session to read books with the children and look at the art gallery.

At the end of the topic, hold an art auction and sell off the children's artwork to parents, carers and friends.

Open a real school library so children can borrow books to take home and read with their families.

Personal, Social and Emotional Development
Ask children to choose a favourite book and tell the group what they like about it. (PS2, 3)

Encourage children to take turns being the librarian and using the scanner (see 'Setting up'). (PS1, 7, 8)

What happens if a library book gets lost or damaged? What will the librarian say and do? (PS4, 6, 9)

Write a letter to the library pretending that it has to be closed due to lack of funds. What will the children do to save their library? (PS1, 2, 4, 6, 12)

Libraries are supposed to be quiet. How will the librarian cope with a noisy customer? (PS7, 9)

We borrow books from libraries. Talk about borrowing, and looking after other people's belongings. (PS9, 12)

Include dual language books in the library so children can experience different languages. (PS13)

Investigate Braille books for partially sighted children. Show the children a book and put one in the library. (PS4, 9)

Communication, Language and Literacy
Encourage children to share books, read to each other and the group. (L3)

Help children to make books for the library. Fold simple zigzag books and retell well-known stories in words and pictures or make up new stories. (L3, 9)

Make a class big book about how to use the library. (L3, 5, 7)

Ask questions and take turns in conversations: 'Have you got any books about Percy the Park Keeper?' 'Yes, they are over here.' (L7, 10)

How will children choose which book to borrow? Look at illustrations, number of words, back cover blurb, recommendation of a friend. Help children to write a simple book review for others to read. (L3, 7, 15, 16)

Make signs for the library: 'Exit', 'Returned books', 'Fines', 'Quiet please'. (L16)

Make library tickets with children's names and bar codes (patterns of thin/thick black lines). (L17)

Compile a catalogue for the art gallery using numbers, titles and names of artists. (L16, 17)

Mathematical Development

Make a big number book for the library. Look at a selection of number books and help children design and make one for the library. (M1, 2, 3, 4)

Decide how many books children are allowed to borrow. 'I have chosen three books. Can I borrow one more?' 'No, you are only allowed two. You will have to put one back!' (M1, 2, 4, 5, 6)

Make a chart of children's favourite books and put it up on the library wall. (M1, 2, 3, 4)

Number the pictures in the art gallery so children can refer to them in the catalogue. Add prices to the pictures. Use really big numbers for fun. 'This picture costs £1,000!' (M1, 3)

Sort books into different sizes. Which is the biggest, smallest, thinnest, thickest, and heaviest? (M9)

'Can I have that book, please. The tall one at the back of the shelf.' (M10)

Knowledge and Understanding of the World

Talk about different types of books – story, board, picture, non-fiction, chapter, pop-up. Invent a simple way of classifying them using shapes, colours or initial letters. (K2, 3, 4)

Talk about how the tickets, scanner and bar codes work. (K4, 7)

Make picture frames for the art gallery using thin strips of dowelling or corrugated card. (K5, 6)

Set up a working computer so children can experiment with word processing in the library. With an adult, search on the Internet for the local library website. (K7)

Use a photocopier to make copies of children's artwork and reduce or enlarge their pictures. Use them in a brochure to advertise the art gallery. (K7)

Ask children if they like the atmosphere in their library. What do they like and what would they change? (K9, 11)

Physical Development

Children need to take care when carrying piles of books around the library and stacking high shelves. (PD1, 2)

Move carefully around the library so that people and books don't get knocked. (PD1, 3)

Covering and mending damaged books requires controlled movements. (PD2, 8)

Open a library delivery service for people who are housebound. Use sit and ride toys to take books to the home corner. (PD2, 6, 7)

Work with clay and junk materials to make sculptures for the art gallery. (PD8)

Creative Development

Paint posters of book characters to hang on the library wall. (C1)

Paint self-portraits for the art gallery. (C1)

Look at the work of one artist such as Mondrian, Picasso or Pollock and paint in their style. Hang the paintings in the gallery. (C1)

Using a variety of printing materials, print repeated patterns on thin strips of card to make frames for artwork in the gallery. (C1)

Be dramatic. Choose a different role: grumpy librarian, noisy child, crazy artist and rude art critic.

Look at illustrations in children's books. Which do the children like best - cartoons, paintings, collage? (C5)

Use a variety of materials to make collage pictures of landscapes to hang in the gallery. (C5)

Campsite

Adapt to include a farm shop

When the weather permits, children benefit from creating and using an outside role-play area such as a campsite. This can be set up inside if there is no suitable grassy area available. It relates to themes on Homes, Holidays, Weather and Summer.

What you will need

For dressing up - suitable outside clothes for cold weather: jackets, jeans, boots, hats, scarves; and for sunny weather: swimsuits, T-shirts and shorts, sunhats, sunglasses

One or more tents, tent pegs, mallet

Sleeping bags

Lilos, inflatable beds

Fold-up chairs, picnic table

Paddling pool, water toys

Camping stove

Cool box – with plastic plates, bowls, cups, pretend and real food

Saucepan

Water containers, empty plastic milk cartons

Rucksacks

Torches

Walking sticks

Maps

Binoculars

Next stop

Open a farm shop or produce stall for the campers to visit.

Provide bread, milk cartons, cheese, vegetables (real and plastic) and eggs.

Things to make and do

Make a fake fire for the campsite using twigs, sticks and red, orange and yellow tissue paper and material.

Build a caravan from screens, big boxes and sheets of cardboard. Cut square windows and doors and paint on wheels. Put fold-up furniture inside and pack everything up in boxes at the end of each day so the whole structure can be moved easily.

Make fruit and vegetables from newspaper, Modroc and paint for the farm shop.

Setting up

Go outside with the children and choose a good pitch. Walk around to find a flat surface, in the shade and not too near the road. With adult help, put up the tent and arrange beds and sleeping bags inside.

Unpack the cool box, cooking things and other furniture.

Set up the farm shop so campers can buy provisions.

Starting off

Invite children to sit in and around the tent in small groups. Introduce the area. Talk about children's experiences of camping. Has anyone slept overnight in a tent on holiday? What is it like?

Read 'Alfie goes Camping' from *The BIG Alfie Out of Doors Story Book* or *Alfie's Weather* by Shirley Hughes (Red Fox).

Safety Don't climb on the tent or try to squeeze too many people inside. Take care not to trip over the guy ropes. Remember when outside to keep away from gates and keep inside boundaries set by the adults.

Roles Campsite manager, events/activities organiser, playleader or kids' club staff, families on holiday.

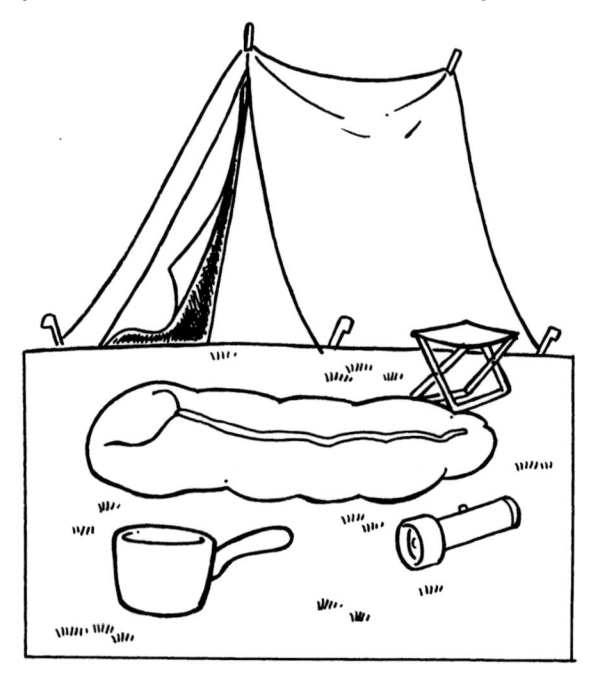

Visits and visitors

Invite an adult who has had lots of experience of camping in different places to come and talk to the children about life under canvas.

Try to borrow a caravan and park it outside for children to explore. Children could have snack and story time in the caravan for a treat.

Visit a pond at the local park or in the school grounds. Try pond dipping using buckets, nets, small plastic cups, and magnifying glasses to examine a catch.

Outside play

Try some bird watching. Use binoculars, sit quietly, and watch birds in the garden. Provide books and photos of birds on laminated sheets so children can identify them. Take photos. Draw sketches of birds.

Build a real campfire outside. Ensure tents and children are a safe distance away. Have buckets of water and sand nearby and set clear rules. Enlist parents if necessary to help with supervision. Sing campfire songs and eat barbecued sausages in hot dog rolls.

On a sunny day set up the paddling pool outside the tent for the campers to enjoy a paddle and a splash.

Home links

Bring in photos of family camping holidays and make a display.

Ask parents to consider taking children camping for a weekend or put up a tent in the back garden and have a picnic.

Personal, Social and Emotional Development

Help children to decide what they would need to pack in a rucksack to spend the night in a tent. Don't forget toothbrushes. (PS1, 4, 7)

Ask children to be sensible about how many people go in the tent at once and to take turns with all the equipment. (PS1, 8)

Talk about keeping safe if the sun is hot outside. Encourage children to wear sunhats and keep in the shade. (PS4, 10)

Talk about different weather conditions. What will they do if it is cold? What happens if it rains when you are camping? Share ideas for a rainy day in a tent. What does it feel like to be safe inside the tent when it's raining outside? (PS4, 6)

Write a letter to the children at the campsite to say that the local council is planning to close the site and build offices on the land. How will the children react? (PS112, 13)

What do the children think it would be like to live in a tent all the time? (PS13)

Communication, Language and Literacy

Tell children real or imaginary stories about 'A noisy night in a tent'. Ask them to help you make up and act out new scary stories. (L3)

The weather is important when you are camping. Make a weather chart for the week to hang in the tent. Sing 'What is the weather today?' from *Bobby Shaftoe, Clap your Hands* (A & C Black). (L3, 5)

Role Play

Invite children to talk to the group about 'A day in a tent'. (L1, 4, 6)

Plan and write a list of what to pack to take camping. 'It might be cold at night. I need a jumper and thick socks!' (L4, 5, 7, 16)

Plan a menu for a day in the tent. What could you cook for each meal? 'I want sausages for breakfast and baked beans on toast for lunch.' (L7, 16)

Help the children to write letters to the council asking them not to close the campsite (see PSED). (L16)

Make up a name for the farm shop. Make a sign and labels for the food. (L15, 17)

Hide name cards around the campsite for children to seek and find. Can they each find three with their name on? (L17)

Mathematical Development

How many children can play safely in the tent? Put up a sign with this number on so that everyone knows. (M1, 2, 3)

Make shopping lists for the farm shop: one loaf of bread, six eggs, three carrots and a litre of milk. (M1, 2, 3)

'You've got two potatoes and I've got two. Is that enough?' (M2, 5, 7)

'We need some more water. Can you carry two containers? Which one is heavier?' (M1, 6, 12)

Use mathematical language. 'Put the water inside the tent.' 'Have you seen the tree behind our tent?' (M10)

Walk around the tent and measure the distance in footsteps. Use hands to measure the height of the tent. (M4, 11, 12)

Leave a container outside the tent to measure rainfall. Record results on a chart. Which was the wettest day? (M4, 12)

Knowledge and Understanding of the World

Encourage children to use all their senses in the campsite: to look at plants and birds, smell the outside air and food cooking, feel what it's like to sleep on the ground, taste camping food and hear the sounds of birds, snoring, traffic and animals. (K1)

Go on a minibeast hunt and make a list of what you find. Look carefully on leaves, bushes and under stones. Take photos. (K2, 7)

Investigate shadows on a sunny day. Can the children lose their shadows? Where is the shadiest place to sit? What shadows can they make with things at the campsite? (K2, 3, 4)

Make miniature folded tents out of cardboard or paper for soft toys to sleep in at the campsite. (K5, 6)

Look at a map of the area and go for a walk with walking sticks, water bottles, snacks and a camera. Take photos of what you see. Go back to the tent and share what you saw. (K4, 7, 9)

Make a plan of the campsite showing where the tents are. Mark exits, play areas, toilets/washing facilities and other buildings. Ask children to use each other's plans to find things. (K9)

What do the children think could improve the campsite? Ask them to help design a play area for the children. (K11)

Physical Development

Organise a 'pack up your tent' race. You will need two tents and a similar amount of clutter to pack in each. Ask children to put all the things carefully inside the tent and zip it up. Who can be ready first? This could be a good way to finish the topic. (PD1, 2, 3, 5)

Try sleeping bag races around the tent. (PD1, 2)

Children have to carry full water containers carefully. Practise pouring drinks for each other. 'Can I have a big drink, please?' (PD1, 2, 6)

Go on a hike with backpacks to the local park or around the outside area. Stop for regular rests and drinks. Do the children notice any changes that happen to their bodies? (PD4, 5)

Use chalk to draw targets on the ground for children to throw balls or beanbags. (PD6)

Creative Development

Make posters to encourage children to protect themselves in the sun by wearing hats and sun lotion. (C1)

Lie in the tent and listen to the sounds outside. What does the rain sound like? Can the children identify all the sounds? Are some of them a bit scary? Use voice, body and instruments to recreate the sounds. (C2, 3)

Be dramatic. It's a stormy night and the tent feels like it's about to be blown away. What can the children do? (C4)

Mime a picnic. Pack all the children's favourite picnic food into a hamper and find a good spot to sit and eat. What could happen to spoil the picnic? (C5)

Make wind chimes to hang on a tree near the tent. Use plant pots, lengths of bamboo or metal piping, old metal forks and spoons, bottle tops and shells. Suspend them on pieces of string or garden wire, hung close together from a branch. The wind should do the rest! Lie in the tent and let the soothing sounds send you to sleep. (C2, 5)

Garden centre

> **Adapt to include a pet's corner/pet shop**

This role-play area could begin with a walk around the local park or garden looking at plants growing in the environment. It is of particular benefit to children who have little experience of caring for a garden and may never have tried to grow plants of their own. It links to themes such as Spring, Growth, Gardens and Easter.

What you will need

For dressing up – overalls, aprons, gloves, boots

Check-out – cash till, money (real and plastic), bags, conveyor belt, chair

Plants – real and homemade

Flowers

Shopping baskets, trolleys

Shelves for displaying goods

Flower pots, seed trays

Tools – trowels, spades and forks

Water sprays

Watering cans

Seed packets

Garden furniture

Gravel, sand, compost

Buckets

Wheelbarrow

Gardening books

Lawn mower

Next stop

Add a pet's corner with lots of soft toy animals.

Add cages, pet food, pet toys, collars and baskets.

Collect together posters of animals and leaflets on animal care.

Set up a real fish tank with a goldfish for the children to help look after.

Things to make and do

Make small pot plants by stuffing a flower pot with shredded brown tissue paper and sticking a colourful tissue or material flower on top.

Make seed packets by cutting up seed or flower catalogues and sticking pictures on small envelopes containing dry rice or beans.

Grow plants from seed such as sunflowers, morning glory, mustard and cress.

Decorate large flower pots or buckets with paint and fill with paper or plastic flowers.

Wrap small boxes or tins in paper and label them cat or dog food for the pet's corner.

Make small pets (mice, hamsters, gerbils) from old grey/brown socks (stuffed with old tights); add buttons for eyes and a felt nose. Build cages for them using Constructo straws.

Role Play

Setting up
Decide with children on different departments for the garden centre. Which will you set up first? Plan ahead for a special day to open the pet's corner.

Set up the check-out with cash till and shopping baskets.

Put plants in seed trays on table. Put seed packets on a display rack. Arrange boots, buckets and tools on the floor.

Starting off
Read *Titch* by Pat Hutchins (Red Fox) or *Doing the Garden* by Sarah Garland (Puffin). Talk about gardens, plants, children and animals growing.

When the pet's corner is open, read *I Want a Cat* by Tony Ross (Red Fox) or *The Three Little Guinea Pigs* by Peter Kavanagh (Little Hippo).

Safety Take care with equipment especially when handling real tools. Handle fragile plants carefully and don't remove from the garden centre. Don't open the seed packets.

Roles Manager, sales assistant, gardener, customer, pet shop assistant, delivery person.

Visits and visitors
Go to a nearby garden centre and let the children observe first hand all the different items for sale. Take clipboards and draw a plan of the garden centre, inside and outside, to use as a guide for your role-play area.

Visit an allotment and watch plants and vegetables growing.

Invite a keen gardener to come and talk to the children about planning and caring for a garden.

Visit a local pet shop in small groups. Ask children to draw pictures of what they saw.

Outside play
Put the climbing and play equipment up outside and pretend it is for sale at the garden centre. Put price labels on the different items. Use large numbers.

Create a mini-pond using a water tray, paddling pool or sandpit liner to display water plants. Float paper and plastic water lilies. Put plastic goldfish and frogs in the water.

Work outside in the nursery or school garden, weeding, planting and watering.

Home links
Ask parents to encourage children to be involved in growing seeds and plants in a pot or in the garden at home. Keep a photo diary of the plants growing.

Take children to visit the local garden centre, flower or pet shop.

Organise a 'Gardener's question time' with parents. Choose a panel and invite parents and children to ask questions about caring for plants. Raise money by selling donated plants and plants from your garden centre at a plant stall.

Personal, Social and Emotional Development
Invite children to talk to the group about 'A day in my life' at the garden centre. (PS1, 2, 3)

Encourage children to share all the equipment and take turns with different roles. If working with pets is the most popular, try introducing a rota so that it is fair. (PS2, 4, 8)

Flowers tend to be bought and given on both happy and sad occasions. When have the children seen a lot of flowers? (PS5, 6)

Somebody who works at the garden centre forgets to water the plants, is always late for work and is rude to the customers. What can the children do? (PS7, 8, 9)

Invite children to dress up and put on protective gloves and boots. Remind them to wash hands after handling plants, compost and animals. (PS10)

One night, a pet escapes from the pet corner. What will the children do? (PS8, 9, 12)

Communication, Language and Literacy
Tell the story of 'Jack and the beanstalk'. Children can role play Jack planting his bean and act out his adventures. (L3, 9, 14)

Work as a group to organise a special opening for the pet's corner. Which pets will be in the shop? What will you need to look after them? Who will work in the shop? (L4, 5, 7)

Enjoy learning names of plants and flowers. Write labels for them. Introduce new words such as compost, gravel, fertiliser. (L8, 17)

Encourage children to use appropriate language. 'Where will I find the bedding plants?' 'Over by the wheelbarrow. Let me show you.' 'Thank you.' (L10)

Provide notices around the garden centre and encourage children to find letters and familiar words. (L11, 13)

Look at plant reference books, leaflets and brochures advertising plants. Can children design a leaflet to promote a newly discovered tree, flower or plant? (L14, 15, 16)

Write shopping lists before going to the garden centre. 'I need a big plant for mum and new boots for me.' (L16)

Make name badges for the staff. (L17)

Mathematical Development

Price plants and other items. Use real 1p, 2p, 5p, 10p coins and count the change. (M1)

Organise a half-price sale. Can the children help work out the new prices? (M1, 2, 3)

Count plants, flowers, pots and pets. Do a stock take and record resources: '8 seed trays, 3 spades, 2 tins of cat food.' (M1, 2, 3)

'How many plants can we fit in this seed tray? Could we fit in one more?' (M4)

'There are three hamsters in that cage and one more in this one. That makes four all together.' (M4, 6)

'There are four daffodils in this bucket. We need one each. There are six of us. How many more will we need?' (M2, 7, 11)

Display plants in an alternating pattern: pansies and marigolds. (M8)

Have a selection of flower pots for children to sort according to size, position, and so on. (M9, 10)

'Can I fit all the plants into my basket?' 'Will I need a bigger car?' (M9, 11)

Make a graph of children's pets to hang up in the pet's corner. (M11)

Fill buckets with wet or dry sand or compost and ask children to lift them. Which is the heaviest? (M12)

Knowledge and Understanding of the World

Encourage children to use all their senses in the garden centre: looking at and smelling flowers, feeling leaves, stroking pets, tasting herbs and vegetables, listening to sounds. (K1)

The manager is worried. 'The plants are not looking very healthy today.' What could the children do to help? (K1, 2, 3, 4)

'What do hamsters like to eat?' Use reference books to find out about plants, pets, food, unusual plants, problems, and so on. (K4)

Ask children to draw pictures to show staff how to care for plants. (K2, 4)

Use the computer to keep a list of all the stock at the garden centre. (K7)

Take photos of real pets and make a display for the pet's corner showing animals and owners, names and ages. (K7, 8)

Ask children to talk to their own families about their gardens. How have they changed recently or over longer periods of time? (K8)

Physical Development

It is important that children learn to carry things safely. Work together to carry heavy buckets, tools and delicate plants. (PD1)

'How shall we stack these plant pots?' 'Can we deliver these plants safely?' Use the sit and ride toys to deliver plants. (PD2, 3)

All put boots on and organise a 'wellie run' outside on the grass! Try another challenge. How far can you throw a boot? (PD1, 2, 3, 6)

Do we need the same things as plants to keep healthy? (PD4)

Handling tools, carrying pets, caring for plants, planting seeds, watering and weeding, all require careful control of movements and awareness of space. (PD3, 6, 8)

Creative Development

Paint pictures of flowers and plants to display at the garden centre. (C1)

Sing and act out 'Mary, Mary, quite contrary, how does your garden grow?' Make up new answering lines. (C2)

Make some garden sounds using plastic flower pots and metal tools from the garden centre. Try shaking gravel in a metal or plastic tray. (C2)

Sing and act out 'I went to the garden centre and bought all the flowers' (adapted from 'I went to the garden', *This Little Puffin*) (C2)

Be dramatic. Go into the garden centre and complain about a plant you bought recently that is now dying. How are the children going to react? (C4)

Paint small flower pots with patterns, flowers and names. Sell them at the plant stall (see 'Home links').

Look at paintings of flowers by artists such as Van Gogh, Monet and Georgia O'Keeffe. Give children a variety of media to produce collage and paintings. Frame the pictures to sell at the garden centre. (C5)

Work in clay to make small flower pots to sell at the garden centre. (C5)

Role Play

Builder's yard

Adapt to an estate agent's

If you're doing a topic on Houses, Homes, Materials or Building, how better to encourage children to extend their learning than opening a builder's merchants or yard in the role-play corner. This could be planned to coincide with building work being done nearby or on site. The children may then decide to turn the role-play area into a building site.

What you will need

For dressing up – overalls, check shirts, jeans, fluorescent waistcoats, boots, hard hats

Bricks – real, plastic, wooden, cardboard boxes

Large sand tray filled with gravel, sand

Planks of wood

Tiles

Pipes

Buckets

Tape measures, rulers

Spirit level

Weighing scales

Tools (real but small size or plastic) - spades, trowels, hammers, saws, nails, screws, nuts and bolts

Decorating equipment – rolls of wallpaper, tins of paint, brushes, paint colour charts, paint trays, ladders

Check-out – cash till, money, pens, chalk, notebooks, squared paper, telephone, directories

Building site – cones, stripy tape to cordon off areas, wheelbarrow, cement mixer, pop-up tent/workman's hut, teapot and mugs, sandwich boxes, building plans

Next stop

Open an estate agent's office. Provide property newspapers and house details.

Set up a desk with telephone, appointment diary, and a big bunch of keys.

Begin to build a new supermarket or the next role-play area on the building site with the children's help (see PSED).

Things to make and do

Collect lots of cereal and large food boxes, stuff with newspaper and tape shut to use as bricks. Cover in plain orange or red sugar paper.

Make windows from cardboard frames and coloured or clear plastic.

Setting up

Sort and display the goods for sale. Put all the building materials on one table, tools on shelves and decorating items on another table.

Set up a table for weighing and measuring items.

Put out a mat and piles of bricks. Children can practise building walls in this area.

Set up a check-out with cash till, baskets, and so on.

Starting off

Read *Miss Brick the Builder's Baby* by Allan Ahlberg (Young Puffin Books) or any Bob the Builder stories and videos.

Safety Take care handling heavy bricks and equipment. Always supervise closely the use of real tools and show children how to use them safely. Advise children not to lift or try to carry anything too heavy.

Roles Manager, sales assistant, customer, builder, foreman, carpenter, electrician, estate agent, house buyer.

Visits and visitors

Ask a parent or adult to come in and show children how walls are built using real bricks, cement and tools.

Visit a working building site and take photos of builders at work.

Go on a walk around the local area and look at different buildings. Compare differences in building materials. Count windows, doors, shapes, and so on.

Outside play

Read *Moving Molly* by Shirley Hughes (Red Fox). Pack up the home corner and move house. Pack everything into big cardboard boxes and wrap things in newspaper and bubble wrap. Transport outside and set up a new home corner. Clean or redecorate the original home corner before you move everything back!

Tape off an area outside and dig a hole in the earth with the children. Wear dressing-up clothes and hard hats.

Home links

Encourage parents to take children to visit the local builder's yards, building site or DIY store.

Ask parents to try and involve children with any DIY or decorating going on at home, for instance choosing new wallpaper for their room.

Personal, Social and Emotional Development

Encourage children to work together in pairs or small groups. 'It's not safe to lift a long plank on your own.' 'The bucket of gravel is too heavy to carry by myself.' (PS2, 4, 8)

Someone gets hurt at the builder's yard when a brick wall falls down. How can the children help? (PS4, 12)

Talk about moving to a new house. What would the children look forward to and what would they worry about? (PS6)

Give children the responsibility of keeping the yard tidy and safe. What rules will they make? What could happen if tools are left lying around? (PS9, 12)

Children should be as independent as possible in selecting how and what they explore in the builder's yard. 'I am going to buy some bricks and a long piece of pipe.' (PS11)

Ask children to bring in a picture of their home. Draw pictures of houses. Make a display for the estate agent's of 'Our homes'. Look at homes from a variety of cultures. (PS13)

Communication, Language and Literacy

Read *A New Room for William* by Sally Grindley (Bloomsbury). Invite children to talk to the group about decorating, moving house or plans for a new room. (L1, 3)

Write shopping lists. 'I need two tins of blue paint, a new window and some bricks.' (L5, 16)

Act out the nursery rhyme 'Humpty Dumpty'. Use a soft toy Humpty or make one from card. (L3, 4, 5, 7)

Extend vocabulary with words such as 'corners', 'edges', 'balance', 'spirit level', 'cement'. (L8)

Explain what DIY stands for and make up new abbreviations. (L11)

Use *Yellow Pages* and local papers to look at adverts for builder's yards and materials. Write an advert for your yard. (L11, 12, 16)

Phone up the builder's yard and make an order. Put children's names on the order. (L1, 4, 16, 17)

Make signs for the different areas of the yard on bright yellow card – 'Caution', 'Men working overhead', 'Danger', 'Hard hats', 'No entry'. (L15, 16)

Mathematical Development

Sort and count nails and screws according to size, colour, and so on. (M1, 2, 4)

Make price labels for goods in the yard. Use 1p, 2p, 5p and 10p. (M1, 3)

Leave an order at the yard for equipment to be delivered to your address: six bricks, two ropes, one bucket. (M1, 3)

Role Play

One child builds a wall or tower using different-sized wooden bricks. Can another child copy it exactly? How many bricks will you need? Can you make it taller? (M2, 4, 8)

'You wanted four planks of wood. We've given you three already, so you need one more.' (M4, 5, 6)

Introduce tape measures and use comparative language for measuring size. 'Mine is the longest plank, look, it's ten.' (M9)

'I need more yellow bricks.' 'Pass me the square brick next to that long one.' (M4, 9)

'Let's build a wall behind there.' 'Put the window here, above this brick.' (M10)

Knowledge and Understanding of the World

Investigate differences between building materials, such as gravel, sand, bricks and wood. 'They're all hard. You can't use sand.' 'Why is glass used for windows?' (K2, 3, 4)

Use Big Builder, Quadro or another large construction toy to make a crane or other equipment to use in the yard. (K5)

Design and make model houses out of junk materials in the builder's yard. 'My house has big windows at the back.' (K5, 6)

Hang ropes off the climbing frame and investigate pulleys, levers and moving heavy weights. (K4, 6)

Use saws, hammers and nails on the woodwork bench to construct shapes to sell at the yard. (K5, 6)

Talk about houses. How many rooms are there in their house or flat? What do they like and dislike about their house? (K9, 11)

Physical Development

Children could work together to carry materials needed to build a structure. 'Pass the bucket down the line.' (PD1, 2, 3)

Use bricks and planks to create a raised walkway to balance along. (PD2, 7)

Help children to build a low wall using real bricks, cement and a spirit level. Alternatively, use wooden bricks and slip (clay and water). (PD2, 6, 8)

Think about how the activity of building and digging makes our bodies feel. (PD5)

Take care when handling tools. 'Hold this still for me while I put a nail in.' (PD8)

Creative Development

Look at architectural drawings. Ask children to design buildings and draw plans for the building yard. Hang their work on the wall. (C1)

Make patterns of contrasting sounds and noises in the yard: bricks banging, sawing, hammering, mixing and digging. (C2)

Sing and act out 'Peter hammers with one hammer'. Change it to 'Lucy builds with one brick'. Can the children think of any new variations? (C2)

Re-enact the story of 'The three little pigs'. Ask children to build houses out of sticks, straw and bricks. Add sound effects. (C2, 5)

Encourage children to use all their senses to explore materials – coldness of wet sand, weight of bricks, sound of gravel and smell of building materials. (C3)

Fairy stories

> Adapt to 'Goldilocks', 'Jack and the Beanstalk', 'Alice in Wonderland'

Characters from fairy stories and nursery rhymes often have distinctive homes and these can be recreated to inspire a wealth of imaginative role-play experiences. Possible themes include Houses and homes, Fairy stories and Growth or maths topics such as Colours and Size.

What you will need
Three bears' cottage
Bear masks, furry tabards or bear suits
Goldilocks dress/plaits on hair band
Home corner kitchen furniture
Bowls and spoons in three sizes
Chairs in three sizes
Beds in three sizes
Saucepan of porridge
Giant's kitchen
False beard, glasses, wig
Large adult-sized clothes, male and female, including slippers, dressing gown, hats and shirts
Broadsheet newspaper
Large table and chairs, mirror, cupboard
Large salad or mixing bowls, wooden spoons
Large teapot, mugs, plates
Giant boxes of food
Big vase of flowers
Queen of Heart's palace
Crowns, tiaras, wigs
Cloaks, robes
Fancy clothes, bridesmaid dresses
Fancy hats, gloves, shoes
Jewellery, rings, chains, medals
Throne
Pictures in gold/silver frames
Rich wallpaper on screens
Special china
Candlesticks, candles
Silver trays
Lace tablecloths
Jam tart trays

Next stop
Other fairy story houses that lend themselves to this treatment are Little Red Riding Hood's grandmother's cottage (large bed, bedding, nightdress, wolf mask, red cloak, basket of food); Sleeping Beauty's castle (turreted castle walls, creepers); the witch's gingerbread house from Hansel and Gretel; the three little pigs' houses (straw, sticks and bricks).

Things to make and do
Giant's kitchen
Make a beanstalk from rolled-up newspaper and green crepe paper leaves.

Cut giant-sized knives and forks from card and spray with silver paint. Make giant plates, cups and saucers from boxes, flowerpots and papier mache.

Make a bag of gold by covering card discs or jam jar lids with gold paint or paper. Make a golden harp from card sprayed gold and string.

Queen of Heart's palace

Cut thick card into battlements and stick to the top of a portable screen.

Make fancy gold frames for windows and mirrors. Cut out gold hearts and stick them onto strips of card or use a heart-shaped sponge to print a repeated pattern.

Role Play

Make a throne by covering a chair with velvet or gold shiny fabric.

Make salt dough jam tarts using red and white dough.

Make a drape by covering a plain light coloured material or old sheet with hearts using fabric pens and paint.

Setting up

Three bears' cottage
Set up kitchen and bedroom areas using the different-sized equipment. To create the effect of going upstairs to the bedroom use some blocks or climbing apparatus to make steps.

Giant's kitchen
Hang the beanstalk on the wall outside the kitchen so that Jack can make a quick get-away.

Paint a huge giant door on the wall and use screens to create walls.

Queen of Heart's palace
Use the castle screens to make a square shaped area. Cover the walls with hearts, painted, cut out, printed, and collage.

Hang the heart drapes like curtains around the throne and other furniture.

Starting off

Read the traditional story or rhyme to introduce the role-play area. Compare different versions of the story. Talk about different roles and the character's home and how you could recreate it.

Safety Take care with giant-sized clothes and furniture.

Roles Goldilocks, three bears, Jack, Jack's mother, giant, giant's wife, Queen of Hearts, king, knave, prince, princess.

Visits and visitors

Invite staff or parents to dress up as a royal visitor, the giant or other fairy story character. Help children to prepare and plan how to make the visit special. Interview the visitor and ask appropriate questions. Take photographs and make a book of 'The day the Queen of Hearts visited our school'.

Outside play

Make a forest of trees for the three bears to walk through. Cut out leaves from green sugar or crepe paper and stick onto newspaper trunks and branches. Stand the trees in weighted down plastic containers.

Make a trail of giant-sized footprints or bear prints. Cut them from plastic or draw with chalk across the outside play area. Can the children follow the trail? Can they stretch their stride to walk in the giant's footsteps?

Home links

Invite parents to tell their children fairy stories from memory.

Ask children to find picture books of different fairy stories and bring them in.

Personal, Social and Emotional Development

Let children be involved in choosing which fairy story character to focus on and whose house or castle to create in the role-play area. (PS1, 7, 8, 11)

Cooperate in a group to take turns with roles, dressing-up clothes and other equipment. Encourage children to work together to re-tell and act out the stories. (PS1, 2, 8)

Share a teddy bears' picnic with the children in the three bears' forest. Make honey sandwiches to eat for a snack. Invite children to bring in a special bear from home to join them at the picnic. Make name labels for the bears. (PS1, 4, 8)

The three bears were upset when they saw the damage Goldilocks had caused. How does it feel when someone breaks something belonging to you? (PS4, 5, 6, 12)

Help children to talk about right and wrong. Should Goldilocks have gone into the three bears' house and used their things? Was Jack right to take the giant's gold? What could the Knave of Hearts do to say sorry? (PS8, 9, 12)

Communication, Language and Literacy

Make a collection of storybooks telling the same fairy story or rhyme. Put them in the house for children to look at and compare. (L1, 3)

Write a new fairy story adventure featuring Baby Bear, Goldilocks or Jack. Use 'Once upon a time' and 'They all lived happily ever after'. (L3, 13, 14)

Work in a group to retell and act out the stories for an audience. Use different voices and think about the feelings of characters. (L3, 4, 6, 7, 9)

Make a set of sequencing pictures for the children to use to retell the story. (L3, 5, 7, 9)

Make a fairy story alphabet to hang up in the role-play area. (L8, 11, 12)

Practise talking properly in the palace. 'When is her majesty returning?' 'Will you require anything else, madam?' 'Thank you, sir.' (L10)

Write a group letter to Goldilocks' mum complaining about her behaviour. (L3, 14, 16)

Write giant-sized notes using a big pencil, paper and letters. (L15, 16)

Write invitations to a party at the palace. 'The Queen of Hearts wishes to invite .... to attend a banquet to celebrate her fifth birthday on Friday at 2 o'clock.' (L16, 17)

Make heart-shaped name badges for guests to wear at the palace. (L17)

Mathematical Development

Set the table at the three bears' house with three different-sized bowls, spoons and chairs. (M1, 2, 3)

Hold a 'Number three' day. Invite children to bring in three things from home in a bag. Look at the number three in stories: three bears, three little pigs, three Billy Goats Gruff. Collect three different-sized bags, balls, shoes, and so on. Eat three pieces of fruit for a snack. (M1, 2, 3, 9)

Count how many golden coins are in the giant's bag. How many leaves are there on the beanstalk? How many eggs has the golden hen laid? (M1, 2)

The Queen of Hearts is having a banquet. She has invited the three bears and Jack and his mother. 'You will need to set the table for six.' 'If the giant comes too you will need one more place.' (M1, 2, 5, 6)

Make royal flags, bunting and banners to decorate the palace using repeated patterns. (M8)

Compare the sizes of the giant's cup and Jack's cup and the three bears' furniture. (M9)

Can you spot where Jack is hiding? 'Behind the curtain', 'Underneath the table', 'Inside the cupboard'. (M10)

Knowledge and Understanding of the World

Cook porridge for the children to try in the three bears' house. Notice how the dry oats change when milk is added. Is it too hot or too cold? (K1, 3, 4)

Grow a beanstalk or plant a sunflower seed. Let the children see how slowly a normal plant grows. (K1, 4, 9)

Cook jam tarts. Have a royal tea party with punch made from cold tea, apple juice and chopped up fruit. (K3, 4, 6)

Take photos of royal visitors, three bears, little Red Riding Hood, the giant and display in a photo album. (K7)

Use a compass to find your way around the three bears' forest. (K7)

What do the children think it would have been like to live in a castle or palace in the past? (K8)

Draw a map of the area including the forest. Can you show Goldilocks the way home, or show the prince where to find Sleeping Beauty? (K9)

Physical Development

Draw a winding path through the three bears' forest (see 'Outside play') using chalk. Ask children to follow the path. Use blue mats as streams for children to wade across or make stepping stones for them to jump onto. (PD1, 2)

Pretend to climb a beanstalk, walk like a giant, run like Jack, plod like the three bears, skip like Goldilocks, and so on. (PD1, 2, 3)

Ask children to use white pieces of paper to lay a trail from the cottage, through the tunnel, up the climbing frame, around the screens, using all the equipment, for a friend to follow. (PD6, 7)

Practise walking regally like a king or queen. Try balancing a bean bag on your head. Use the balance beam. Organise a wedding or coronation procession. (PD1, 7)

Creative Development

Paint portraits of different fairy story characters to frame and hang in the house. (C1)

Sing and act out 'When Goldilocks went to the house of the bears,' and 'There was a princess long ago.' (C2)

Use high and low voices for Jack and the giant. Play high and low notes on a xylophone or keyboard to accompany their footsteps. Make Jack move faster than the giant's slow steps. (C2)

Be dramatic. Make up new endings for the fairy stories. Could Goldilocks make friends with Baby Bear? (C4, 5)

Read funny versions of the story such as *Jim and the Beanstalk* by Raymond Briggs (Puffin) and *Three Little Wolves and the Big Bad Pig* by Eugene Trivizas (Heinemann). Let children act out the new versions. (C4, 5)

Make crowns from gold card and collage materials. (C5)

Make bear masks out of card and fun fur to wear in the three bears' house. (C5)

Undersea world

This role-play experience uniquely combines the reality of a beach area with a seaside shop and sand and water activities alongside the more fantasy based undersea world created one step away through a simple dividing curtain. It fits well with the themes of Water, Sea, Holidays and Homes.

What you will need

For dressing up – mermaid tails, flippers, masks, wet suits, oxygen tanks, swimsuits

Undersea area – blue fabric, plastic sheeting, green garden netting, green and brown crepe paper, blue mats, pebbles, shells, rocks

Soft toys or plastic sea creatures

Treasure chest, jewels

Lighthouse (see 'Things to make and do')

Beach area – yellow mats, dry sand, shells

Sand and water trays

Large fruit and vegetable boxes (for boats)

Seaside shop – sunhats, sun lotion, sunglasses, flip-flops, swimwear, buckets and spades, toy boats, fishing nets, inflatable toys, swim rings, armbands, ice creams, lollies, sticks of rock, fancy shells, cash till, money

Things to make and do

Build a lighthouse using big boxes at the base and then a tower of cylindrical paint tubs. Cover with paper and paint with red and white stripes. Place a bicycle lamp or camping lamp at the top!

Make ice creams using balls of newspaper wrapped in coloured Cellophane or tissue paper and popped in cones made from cardboard.

Paint thin cardboard tubes pink or green and wrap in Cellophane to make sticks of rock.

Cut card into lolly shapes, paint with a mixture of paint and glue, stick on a lolly stick and dip into hundreds and thousands.

Make oxygen tanks for divers using large plastic drink bottles strapped together.

Setting up

Place the lighthouse in the corner between beach and undersea area.

Put blue mats down for the undersea area and cover with pebbles, shells, soft toys, fishes and treasure chest.

Put down a yellow mat and sprinkle with dry sand for the beach area. Put a sand tray on the beach so children can play with the sand.

Hang up green netting from ceiling hooks as a curtain between the two areas. If possible, put net over the top to make a roof. Suspend ribbons of crepe paper from the netting like seaweed.

Line a water tray with a dark plastic bin liner to create a rock pool. Put in sand, small rocks, shells, and plastic sea creatures. Use small fishing nets to catch creatures.

Starting off

Watch excerpts from the Disney video *The Little Mermaid*.

Read contrasting stories *The Fish who Could Wish* by John Bush (OUP), *Who are You? In the Sea* by Vic Parker (Franklin Watts) and *Lucy and Tom at the Seaside* by Shirley Hughes (North-South).

Talk about children's own experiences of the seaside, beach and swimming or paddling in the sea.

Safety Don't hang on the net. Take care moving around wearing flippers and mask. Avoid snorkels, as they would be unhygienic.

Roles Mermaid, deep-sea diver, fisherman, swimmer, holidaymaker, families, lighthouse keeper, shopkeeper, lifeguard.

Visits and visitors

If you live near the sea, arrange for children to spend some time at the beach and make a list of what will be needed to stock the shop and undersea area.

Invite any adults who have experienced living by or on the sea to visit and talk to the children – lighthouse keeper, sea fisherman, sailor, beach comber.

Outside play

On a fine day, put a paddling pool outside for the children to enjoy. They can buy things from the seaside shop to play with in the water.

Move the water tray rock pool and sand trays outside.

Home links

Ask parents to bring in holiday photos of children and their families at the beach. What different things do children get up to at the beach?

Ask if any family has a pet goldfish or tropical fish

aquarium that they could lend to you for the children to observe and care for.

Open an ice cream stall on a hot day with ice cream cornets, vanilla ice cream, and lots of toppings. Sell ice creams to raise funds.

Personal, Social and Emotional Development

Read *The Rainbow Fish* by Marcus Pfister (North-South Books). Ask children to act out the story in the undersea area. Talk about sharing. How does it feel if someone refuses to share? (PS2, 3, 4, 9)

Encourage children to share the popular equipment and dressing-up outfits. (PS1, 7, 8)

What would happen if someone at the beach was stung by a jellyfish or chased by a shark? Who could help? (PS2, 4)

Serve real ice lollies for a special snack on the beach. Make small lollies by freezing fruit juice in empty fromage frais pots. (PS4, 6)

Children could work together as a team. Set them a challenge to find where the mermaid has hidden her treasure. Help them to take turns with the equipment and in suggesting ideas. (PS8)

Encourage children to choose and put on swimsuits and dressing-up clothes. Some may prefer to put them on over their day clothes. (PS10, 11)

Communication, Language and Literacy

Read *The Lighthouse Keeper's Lunch* by Ronda and David Armitage (Scholastic). Retell and act out the story. Fix a length of string between the top of the lighthouse and the beach for the basket of food to slide down. (L3, 7, 9)

Children could imagine a day on the beach or under the sea and show and tell the group what happens. (L1, 4, 5, 6)

Write a report about the beach for the newspaper. 'The water is clean. There is no litter. But it is very noisy!' (L7, 8, 16)

Look in non-fiction books to find out about sea creatures. Draw pictures of unusual deep-sea fish and hang them on the walls of the undersea area. Extend vocabulary by learning their names. (L8, 14)

Make signs and labels for different items in the 'Seashore shop'.

Collect lots of 'sh' words. Try saying the tongue twister 'She sells seashells on the seashore...' (L1, 2, 8, 11)

Mathematical Development

'Who wants an ice cream?' Count the children to find out how many ice creams to buy. (M1, 2)

Do a stock take in the shop. 'How many sticks of rock are there?' 'We need lots more buckets and spades.' (M1, 2, 4)

Use 1p, 2p, 5p, and 10p price labels in the shop. (M1, 3)

Role Play

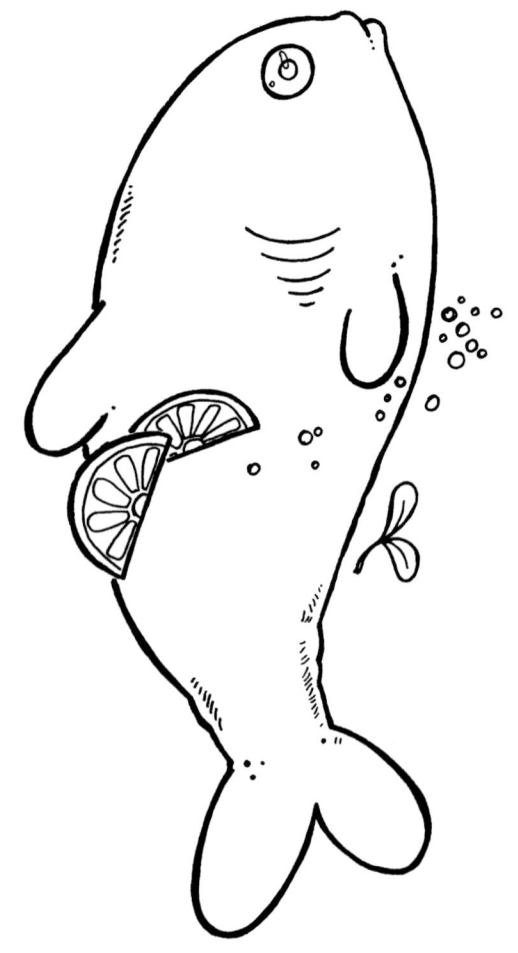

How much will two ice creams cost? Have you got enough money? (M1, 2, 5, 11)

Use large boxes as fishing boats. Cut out card fish shapes and decorate. Add metal paper-clips. Challenge children to catch as many fish as they can using a rod with a magnet on the end. 'Can you catch one more? How many have you caught all together?' (M1, 2, 4, 5)

'I want two ice creams and two lollies, please.' (M5, 7)

Design a patterned beach towel or windbreaker using bright colours and shapes. (M8)

Knowledge and Understanding of the World

Look at a whole fish or crab using a magnifying glass. Feel the scales or skin. Cook it. Enjoy the smell and taste. Compare with fish fingers! (K1, 3)

Investigate floating and sinking in the rock pool. Help children to draw a chart of which things they think will float or sink. 'Can you find three things that float?' (K1, 4)

Fold simple origami paper boats to float in the rock pool. (K4, 5)

Construct boats from off-cuts of soft balsa wood, straws, card, material sails, nails and string. Will they float in the rock pool? (K5, 6)

Talk about beach holidays in the past. Look at old photographs. What did people wear to go into the sea? (K8)

Look at pictures of beach huts. Design and build a beach hut for the children to change in. Use screens, cereal boxes, and sheets of card, paint and a corrugated card roof. (K5, 6, 8)

Encourage children to use all their senses. Think about what the beach or undersea world might smell, look, taste, feel and sound like. What do they like and dislike? What could be improved? (K1, 11)

Physical Development

Ask children to move in the undersea area like different sea creatures - crabs, eels, octopuses, and big shoals of fish. (PD1, 3)

How many of the children can swim? Invite them to lie on their stomachs and practise swimming moves. Organise swimming races. (PD2, 3, 5)

Use large vegetable or fruit boxes as boats. Ask children to practise rowing moves and try to move across the floor. (PD1, 2, 3, 6)

Play throwing and catching games with a large inflatable beach ball or ring. (PD6)

Read *The Sand Horse* by Ann Turnbull (Red Fox). Use the sand tray on the beach to make sand sculptures and castles using buckets and spades. (PD6, 8)

Use small fishing nets to catch creatures in the rock pool. (PD6, 8)

Creative Development

Paint large underwater scenes using white candles, wax crayons and blue paint wash. Use to decorate undersea walls. (C1)

Draw around the outlines of two children and paint them wearing old-fashioned swimwear. Cut out the faces and leave a frame so other children can look through and have funny seaside photographs taken. (C1)

Listen to taped sounds of the seaside and use instruments and vocal sounds to recreate them. How do you make a seagull sound? (C2)

Make watery background sounds using rainsticks, bottles, shakers half full of coloured water and maracas. (C2, 3)

Be dramatic. A boat gets into difficulty on the sea. How will the children help? (C4)

Make jellyfish from semi-circles of bubble wrap and strips of Cellophane or ribbon. Hang them up in the undersea area. (C5)

Bear cave

> **Adapt to a pirate cave or Nativity scene**

Children love exploring and making dens. A bear cave, made from screens, drapes, boxes and whatever else is available, provides endless opportunities for hiding, hibernating, and cosy home building. It can fit into several topics – 'Dark and light', 'Homes', 'Habitats' and 'Winter' or can be inspired by picture books such as *Can't you Sleep, Little Bear?* by Martin Waddell and the Mr Bear stories by Debi Gliori.

What you will need

For dressing up – furry tabards, hats, gloves, and slippers, or complete bear outfit

Bear puppets

Screens, big boxes, pieces of corrugated card

Dark fabric drapes, blankets

Climbing frame

Discovery boxes - Small boxes containing different things for children to observe, draw, and find out about:

Wood - logs, bark, driftwood, branches

Rocks – varying size, weight, texture, colour, patterns

Natural objects – cones, seeds, shells, sponges

Leaves – different sizes, colours, shapes, and leaf skeletons

Magnifying glasses, boxes

Night-time animals – furry, plastic, inflatable

Bats, spiders, cobwebs

Bedding and chairs for bears

Torches, lanterns

Tape recorder

Clipboards, pencils

Food for a hibernating bear

Build a pirate ship and provide dressing-up clothes including hats, patches, bandanas, stripy jumpers, parrots and curtain rings to hang over ears as ear-rings.

At Christmas, change it into the stable at Bethlehem and re-enact the Nativity story.

Things to make and do

Paint the outsides of cardboard boxes, cover with paper leaves and creepers.

Find pictures of animals that live in caves.

Draw, paint and cut out animal footprints.

Make lanterns using different-sized boxes. Cut out windows in all four sides of the boxes and stick on yellow Cellophane. Add a folded card handle.

Make cobwebs by drizzling PVA glue onto round margarine lids in a cobweb pattern. Sprinkle with glitter. Leave to dry, peel off lid and hang up in the cave.

Next stop

Once the bears have moved out, the children could decide what to use the cave for next – pirates and treasure, smugglers, other animals, children on a treasure island, and so on.

Setting up

Choose a corner in the room for the cave. Stack the painted cardboard boxes on their sides, with the openings facing inwards and stick or staple them together to make walls. This creates lots of nooks and

Role Play

crannies for hiding things inside the cave.

Alternatively, cover the climbing frame with dark drapes to make a cave space.

Make the entrance quite small so that the interior remains dark. Use a play tunnel to encourage children to crawl into the cave. Be careful that children with mobility problems can still use the cave with help, perhaps by moving the tunnel when necessary.

Decorate the inside with more leaves, creepers, animal footprints and pictures of cave animals.

Scatter wood, rocks and stones on the floor of the cave.

Play a tape of water dripping as a sound effect.

Stick 'glow in the dark' stars on the wall outside the cave.

Add furniture and accessories for the bears as required, depending on how authentic you want it to be.

Starting off
Talk about different homes, habitats and hibernation. Let the children decide with you if the cave area is going to be realistic or fantasy based.

Gather children in and around the cave to read *Can't you Sleep, Little Bear?* by Martin Waddell.

Safety Don't attempt to climb the walls or the climbing frame while they are disguised as a cave! Handle any living creatures, even minibeasts, with care and respect.

Roles Bears of different sizes, family members, for example Mummy, Daddy and Baby Bear.

Outside play
Read *We're Going on a Bear Hunt* by Michael Rosen (Walker). Re-enact the story outside with the children, moving through grass, trees, mud, snow, and so on, until they reach the bear cave (inside).

Go on a minibeast hunt outside. Where do the creatures like to hide? Which minibeasts would the children expect to find in a cave?

Home links
Check with parents if children have any particular fear of the dark, animals or minibeasts.

Ask parents to show children the night sky, pointing out different stars and the moon. Talk about how it feels in the dark, inside and outside.

Talk to children and parents about bedtime routines. Organise a Pyjama Day and invite children to come to nursery with their pyjamas and slippers and take it in turns to sleep in the cave. Have hot chocolate and cookies for snack.

Personal, Social and Emotional Development
Children will enjoy working together to construct the cave and then using it cooperatively as an imaginative play environment. (PS1, 8)

Ask children to re-enact the story *Can't you Sleep, Little Bear?* in the cave. Does Big Bear get angry when Little Bear can't sleep? Do the children ever have trouble getting to sleep at night? What helps them: counting sheep, singing songs, and listening to story tapes? (PS2, 3, 4, 8)

Talk about feeling afraid of the dark. Be sensitive to any children who express this fear. What else are the children afraid of? How can they help each other? (PS2, 3, 4, 6)

Does there need to be a limit on how many children can play in the cave? Can the children organise a system? (PS4, 7, 8, 9)

Put different activities inside the cave in nooks and crannies for children to discover and select. (PS1, 2, 11)

Communication, Language and Literacy
Re-enact the bear hunt (see 'Outside play') and make up new places for the children to go. Who will be the bear waiting in the cave? (L1, 2, 3)

Listen to taped stories in the dark cave. (L3)

Invite child to role play Big Bear, and read or tell scary stories from the Big Bear chair in the cave. (L3, 9)

Children could imagine 'A day in the life of a bear waking up from a long winter sleep'. (L4, 5)

Children can choose words to describe different bears and make badges such as hairy bear, scary bear, little bear, grumpy bear, kind bear, and so on. (L11, 12, 16)

Find out about bears and other hibernating animals from non-fiction books. (L14, 15)

Make a group flap book about a bear hiding in the cave. (L3, 14, 16)

Write invitations from the bear family to another bear or other animal to come and visit. (L16, 17)

Write a list of what the bear needs to get ready before hibernating through the winter. (L16)

Mathematical Development

In pairs, re-enact the story of *Can't you Sleep, Little Bear?* using different-sized lanterns. (M1, 2, 9)

Count rocks, stones and pebbles in the cave. Sort and order them according to size, colour and weight. (M1, 2, 12)

Share out the winter food fairly. 'There are four bears in here and four fishes to eat. Can we have one each?' (M1, 2, 11)

Put up a sign saying how many children can play in the cave at once. (M3)

'Only four are allowed to play in the cave.' 'There are three of us in here now. Only Tom can come in.' (M2, 5, 6)

Draw repeating patterns on the cave wall using white fabric paint on the dark drapes. (M8)

'Put that box at the top, next to the long thin one'. 'Is there anything hiding behind that rock?' (M10)

Knowledge and Understanding of the World

Put discovery boxes in the cave wall with different things inside for the children to use all their senses to investigate (see 'What you will need'). Change these each week to keep the children involved and stimulated. (K1)

Try putting minibeasts from the hunt in magnifying boxes in the cave. Use magnifying glasses to look closely at rocks, shells, sponges, and wood. (K1, 2)

Look in reference books to find out about caves. How are they formed? What creatures live in them? (K2, 4, 9)

Organise a torch day. Invite children to bring in a labelled torch from home. Talk about how the torches work. Take the torches into the cave and shine them on the walls. (K1, 4, 7, 9)

How dark can you make the cave using boxes and drapes? What could you do to make it even darker? (K4, 5)

Encourage children to be involved in building the cave and keeping it in one piece while playing in it. (K5, 6)

Physical Development

Try some torch dancing. In the cave or a darkened room, shine torches on the ceiling and dance to spooky night music. (PD1)

Crawling in and out of the cave through the tunnel or small entrance will require care and coordination. (PD2)

Be aware of limited space inside the cave and move around carefully so as not to hurt anyone else or damage the structure. (PD1, 2, 3)

Why do bears sleep through the winter? Why do we need sleep? (PD4)

Ask children to move like big grizzly bears in and out and around the cave. (PD1, 7)

Handling rocks, bark, fragile leaves, and minibeasts require careful control and coordination of movements. (PD2, 6)

Sing and act out 'The bear walked over the mountain' (*This Little Puffin*). (PD1, 2, 7)

Make small model caves out of clay and use small plastic bears to play in them. Re-enact a scene from the role-play area. (PD6, 8)

Creative Development

Make press prints of simple human figures or stick men in the style of prehistoric cave drawings and hang them up in the cave. (C1)

Make observational drawings of rocks, shells, bark, leaves and so on. (C1)

Feel the different textures of rocks, stones, and bark. Do rubbings using wax crayons, chalk and thin paper. (C1, 3)

Play the listening game 'Mrs Bear lives in a cave' from *Bobby Shaftoe, Clap your Hands* (A & C Black). (C2, 3)

Be dramatic. Choose different moods for the bear that lives in the cave – angry, tired, sad, jealous, kind, brave. Can the children act out and guess how the bear is feeling? (C4, 5)

Put musical instruments in the cave and invite children to create 'cave compositions' or 'night music'. (C5)

Make bear masks out of card and fun fur to wear in the cave. (C4, 5)

Role Play

Space rocket

Let the children's imagination combine with yours in creating an 'out of this world' fantasy role-play area that they will use again and again to explore space and travel. It works well with a Space theme, or topics on Homes, Where we live and Opposites.

What you will need

For dressing up - space suits (shop bought), shell suits, shiny track suits, helmets, silver foil/material tabards, oxygen tanks, Wellington boots (sprayed silver), padded gloves

Dark drapes, curtains

Sheets/rolls of silver foil or mirrored plastic

Bubble wrap, corrugated card

Large boxes

Computer screen

Old electronic mixing desk or equipment

Telescope

Binoculars, cameras

Empty plastic bottles, plastic tubing

Bottle lids

Play microwave

Swivel office chairs, pretend seatbelts

Box drinks, bottles with straws

Packets of food

Beds

Torches

Cogs, wheels, construction toys

Things to make and do

Build rocket control panels. Spray boxes with silver paint, stick on CDs for dials, or use card circles and split pins, and bottle lids for lights and buttons. Make levers set in slots using lolly sticks and ping-pong balls. Add numbers and words to the panel.

Make windows from sheets of black sugar paper and silver card frames. Stick on stars and planets to make a space scene.

Make sachets of dry space food using folded paper, stuffed with dry rice/lentils and stapled or taped shut. Help children to think of suitable names for the food.

Make oxygen tanks from empty plastic bottles and plastic tubing. Attach ribbons or Velcro so children can wear them on their backs.

Setting up

Hang drapes or use screens to enclose a corner of the room. Alternatively use the climbing frame as a rocket. Line with suitable space materials (see above).

Position a ladder so children have to climb into the rocket.

Put in control panels all around.

Stick windows up so that children can pretend to look out into space as they travel.

Use play microwave and furniture to create a communal sitting and eating area in the rocket.

Starting off

Talk about films and TV programmes the children may have seen about space. What do they think it would be like inside a space rocket?

Show children a video of the moon landing or rocket launches.

Read *Roaring Rockets* by Tony Mitton (Kingfisher) or *Albie and the Space Rocket* by Andy Cutbill (Collins) to help set the scene.

Safety Take care walking and climbing in dressing-up clothes.

Roles Captain, astronaut, pilot, robot (android), alien.

Visits and visitors
Invite an adult who has a telescope and experience of astronomy to come and talk to the children about stargazing. What can they see through the telescope? Relate this to the stars children can see out of the window of the space rocket.

Outside play
Make the outside area into the surface of another planet. What is the new planet called? Put out rocks and upturned flowerpots with things hidden under them. Encourage children to climb around and see what they can find. What's hiding behind that blue rock? Is it an alien?

Home links
Invite parents and grandparents to share their memories of the moon landing with the children. What were you doing when Neil Armstrong walked on the moon?

Ask parents to show children the night sky and point out the moon and any recognisable star formations.

Personal, Social and Emotional Development
Talk about space, and what the children imagine it would be like to travel in a rocket. How would it feel to be miles away from home, exploring new planets and stars? (PS1, 2, 4, 6)

Ask children to take turns dressing up in the space suits, using the control panels and taking the role of captain. (PS1, 8)

Encourage independence in dressing up and putting on suits, helmets and gloves. Ask children to help each other put on oxygen tanks and pull off boots. (PS4, 10)

What would happen if the rocket broke down in space? How could it be repaired? Could the children work together to solve the problem? (PS2, 4, 6, 8)

Imagine meeting an alien from out of space. Read *Q Pootle 5* by Nick Butterworth (Picture Lions). What would the children do? How would they communicate? (PS4, 5, 9, 12)

Communication, Language and Literacy
Make up stories about adventures in space. Write and illustrate these in a class book. (L3, 16)

Invite girls and boys to take turns at being captain, and 'give orders' to crew. 'First, I want you to take us to this planet.' 'Then can you....' (L4, 5)

Imagine 'A day in space' and relate to the group what might happen to you in the rocket, on the planet surface and on the way home. (L1, 4, 5, 6)

Make signs for the rocket: 'No entry', 'Danger', 'Oxygen', 'Exit', 'Red alert', 'Put on your space suit'. (L13, 17)

Find out about rockets and space travel from non-fiction books. Put books in the rocket so they can be referred to during role play. (L14)

Help children to write down dates and events in the captain's log or diary. Use paper and computer. (L16)

Make name and rank badges for crew to wear. (L16, 17)

Mathematical Development
Count lights and buttons on control panel. 'When those two red lights flash, it means trouble!' 'If the green one comes on, we can go faster.' (M1, 2)

'How many planets and stars can you see out of the window?' (M1, 2)

'The rocket needs more fuel. Put in three more litres, please.' (M1, 2, 3, 4)

Role Play

'Move the dial to number two and switch the lever to number seven'. (M1, 3)

Write out numbers and letters to plot the rocket's route to the next planet or destination. 'Plot a course to Mars, 35K 2900X.' (M1, 3)

Put up a sign saying how many children can play in the space rocket together. (M3)

Compare sizes of stars and planets on the space charts (see Creative Development). 'Let's go to that small one over there, behind the big one with rings. It's very far away.' (M9, 10, 11)

Knowledge and Understanding of the World

Imagine using all the senses in the space rocket. What would it look like in space? What new things would you see and feel? How would it feel to float everywhere? Does it smell of anything in space? What would you expect to hear? (K1, 4)

'We need to go faster to escape the meteor storm.' How does the rocket engine work? What will make it go faster? (K2, 3, 4)

Set up an engineering department in the rocket. Use real screwdrivers and allow children to take apart and investigate old electrical and electronic equipment. Can they draw diagrams of what they see? Put the pictures in a book or repair manual to use in the rocket. (K1, 2, 4, 7)

Make telescopes, binoculars and cameras from painted cardboard tubes and boxes and use them to look at the stars through the window of the rocket. (K4, 5, 6)

Make walkie-talkie radios for the astronauts using small boxes, black paint, PVA glue, straws and buttons. (K5, 6)

Use the computer to store information on the crew and all missions. (K7)

Work in pairs to draw a plan of the rocket. Where does the crew sleep? How could the rocket be improved? (K9, 11)

Physical Development

Go on a space walk outside the rocket wearing space suit, helmet and boots. Pretend to float through space. (PD1, 2, 3)

Try some moonwalking. Imagine gravity boots make it hard to lift your feet inside the rocket but outside you can take giant leaps. (PD1, 2)

Use sit and ride toys as space buggies and ride around the planet surface looking for rare rocks. (PD3, 6)

Pick up moon rocks from the planet surface in big padded gloves. Pretend they are heavy to carry. (PD6)

Can you repair the rocket? Go outside in the space suit and use tools to mend a hole in the outer layer. (PD6)

Attach a tunnel to the rocket so the crew have to crawl through to get in and out. Then ask them to climb across or up the ladder. (PD7)

Creative Development

Paint space pictures or charts on black paper using silver and gold pens or wax crayons. Hang these up in the rocket so crew can use them as maps to find their way to different planets, galaxies and stars. (C1)

Ask children to make sounds of machines in the rocket using voices or instruments. Make long hissing, whirring, bleeping sounds. Record these and use as background noise in the rocket. (C2)

Sing and act out 'Spaceship to the moon' in *Bobby Shaftoe, Clap your Hands* (A & C Black). (C2)

Be dramatic. You are lost in space and don't know how to get home. How will the crew react? (C4, 5)

Make collage stars using shiny materials and glitter to hang outside the rocket. (C5)

Make model planets using balloons, papier mache and paint. Hang the finished planets outside the rocket window. (C5)

Role Play

Role Play